REA's Books Are The Best...

They have rescued lots of grades and more!

(a sample of the hundreds of letters REA receives each year)

"Your books are great! They are very helpful, and have upped my grade in every class. Thank you for such a great product."

Student, Seattle, WA

"Your book has really helped me sharpen my skills and improve my weak areas. Definitely will buy more."

Student, Buffalo, NY

"Compared to the other books that my fellow students had, your book was the most useful in helping me get a great score."

Student, North Hollywood, CA

"I really appreciate the help from your excellent book. Please keep up your great work."

Student, Albuquerque, NM

"Your book was such a better value and was so much more complete than anything your competition has produced (and I have them all)!"

Teacher, Virginia Beach, VA

(more on next page)

(continued from previous page)

"Your books have saved my GPA, and quite possibly my sanity. My course grade is now an 'A', and I couldn't be happier."

Student, Winchester, IN

"These books are the best review books on the market. They are fantastic!"

Student, New Orleans, LA

"Your book was responsible for my success on the exam. . . I will look for REA the next time I need help."

Student, Chesterfield, MO

"I think it is the greatest study guide I have ever used!"

Student, Anchorage, AK

"I encourage others to buy REA because of their superiority. Please continue to produce the best quality books on the market."

Student, San Jose, CA

"Just a short note to say thanks for the great support your book gave me in helping me pass the test . . . I'm on my way to a B.S. degree because of you !"

Student, Orlando, FL

C++

By David Hunter, Ph.D.
Professor of Computer Science
Mary Washington College, Fredericksburg, Va.

And the Staff of
Research & Education Association
Dr. M. Fogiel, Director

Research & Education Association
61 Ethel Road West
Piscataway, New Jersey 08854

SUPER REVIEW®
OF C++

Printed in the United States of America

Library of Congress Control Number 2002112222

International Standard Book Number 0-87891-181-2

II-1

WHAT THIS Super Review WILL DO FOR YOU

This **Super Review** provides all that you need to know to do your homework effectively and succeed on exams and quizzes.

The book focuses on the core aspects of the subject, and helps you to grasp the important elements quickly and easily.

Outstanding **Super Review** features:

- Topics are covered in logical sequence
- Topics are reviewed in a concise and comprehensive manner
- The material is presented in student-friendly language that makes it easy to follow and understand
- Individual topics can be easily located
- Provides excellent preparation for midterms, finals and in-between quizzes
- In every chapter, reviews of individual topics are accompanied by Questions **Q** and Answers **A** that show how to work out specific problems
- Written by professionals and test experts who function as your very own tutors

Dr. Max Fogiel
Program Director

CONTENTS

12 MISCELLANEOUS C++ TOPICS

CHAPTER 1

Language Fundamentals

1.1 Language Overview

C++ is a superset of the C language that incorporates the features of object-oriented programming. With the exception of those language features directly related to object-oriented programming, the two languages are almost identical. This book assumes no prior knowledge of C. In an effort to keep the text as tightly focused as possible, no attempt has been made to clarify the points at which the two languages diverge. In order to familiarize the reader with the structure of the language, an annotated C++ program is presented in Table 1.1.

The language provides two ways of specifying comments. Groups of lines may be marked as comments by bracketing them with the symbols '`/*`' and '`*/`'. Alternately, the symbol '`//`' marks the beginning of a comment restricted to a single line. This is the preferred method.

A C++ program need not conform to a rigid outline. Variable declarations, type definitions, and function definitions may appear in any order, provided that identifiers are declared before they are referenced. Typically, however, a C++ source file begins with a number of preprocessor directives (explained in subsequent chapters). Global type and variable definitions typically come next, followed by any number of function definitions. A C++ executable source file must contain a function called `main()`. Execution, or the start of the program, begins with this function.

TABLE 1.1
An Annotated C++ Program

```
//compiler directives always begin with #
//and are typically placed at the top of a
//file

//include the I/O functions
#include <iostream.h>

//define a constant
#define PI 3.1415927

//A function that, given a radius, returns
//the circumference of a circle
float circum(float radius)
{
  return 2*PI*radius;
}

//The main () function
void main()
{
  float r;                    //local variables
  char c = 'y';
  while (c =='y')
  {
//output newline, prompt, and read r
    cout << "\nEnter the radius of the circle: ";
    cin >> r;

//output result, and prompt to continue
    cout << "The circumference is:"
         << circum(r) << '\n';
    cout << "Enter y to continue, n to exit:";
    cin >> c;
  }
}
```

Identifiers in C++ may be of any length, must start with a letter, and can contain any combination of letters, digits, and the underscore '_' character. The semicolon is used as a statement separator and braces '{ }' to group statements.

C++ is case sensitive. Thus, the strings "SUM", "Sum", and "sum" all represent distinct identifiers. The reserved words of the language must be given in lower case. A complete set of reserved words is presented in Table 1.2.

TABLE 1.2
C++ Reserved Words

asm	auto	break	case
catch	char	class	const
continue	default	delete	do
double	else	enum	extern
float	for	friend	goto
if	inline	int	long
new	operator	private	protected
public	register	return	short
signed	sizeof	static	struct
switch	template	this	throw
try	typedef	union	unsigned
virtual	void	volatile	while

1.2 Primitive Types

The simple types provided by C++ are: `int` for integers, `float` or `double` for real numbers, and `char` for characters. The distinction between `float` and `double` is machine dependent, but generally the `double` type occupies more storage and allows for greater accuracy of representation than does `float`.

Other primitive types can be produced by prefacing the simple types with the keywords `short`, `long`, `signed`, and `unsigned`. This produces types such as `long unsigned int`, `signed char`, and so forth. `Signed` types can store both positive and negative numbers while `unsigned` types store only non-negative values. Consequently, `unsigned` types can store a larger range of non-negative integers than can signed types. All integer and real types are by default signed, while character types are by default `unsigned`.

The meaning of the `short` and `long` modifiers is implementation dependent. Generally, however, `long` types occupy more storage than `short` types but can store a larger range of values.

It is possible to omit the word `int` from a type description. Thus, the type indication `long` is equivalent to `long int`, and the indication `unsigned` is equivalent to `unsigned int`.

1.3 Constants

Integer constants are expressed in the usual manner: 0, 1234, -98, etc. A constant beginning with "0x" is an integer expressed in hex notation: 0x0, 0xfab5, 0x056a, etc.

Real number constants begin with a digit and contain a decimal point followed by digits. They are of type `double` by default. `float` constants may be specified by affixing an "f", as in "3.141592f".

Character constants are specified using single quotes. Non-printable characters are expressed using backslash sequences. These are presented in Table 1.3. Despite their appearance, these *escape sequences* are treated as single characters.

TABLE 1.3
Special Character Constants

Expression	Meaning
`\0`	ASCII null (00 hex)
`\n`	newline
`\t`	horizontal tab
`\v`	vertical tab
`\b`	backspace
`\r`	carriage return
`\f`	form feed
`\?`	question mark
`\a`	audible bell
`\\`	backslash
`\"`	double quote
`\'`	single quote
`\ooo`	octal character code
`\xhhh`	hex character code

The \ooo sequence allows characters to be specified as a one-, two-, or three-digit octal number. There is no limit to the number of hex digits that may be specified using the \x sequence. In either case, a sequence of hex or octal digits is considered to terminate at the first character that is not a legitimate digit of the specified base.

Character strings are specified using double quotes. Non-printable characters can be embedded in strings as shown in the examples below.

```
"Attention!\a\a Attention!"
"Hello World\n"
"\fPage #"
```

The use of character strings in C++ programming is fully explored in a subsequent chapter.

Problem Solving Example:

Using the example program in Table 1.1 as a guide, write a C++ program that prompts the user to enter a non-negative integer and then prints out the factorial of the integer. The program should then ask if the user wishes to repeat the program. Implement a factorial function as part of your program.

A

```
#include <iostream.h>

unsigned long factorial(int n)
{
 int i = n;
 int result = 1;
 while (i > 1)
 {
  result = result*i;
  i = i - 1;
 }
 return result;
}
void main()
{
```

```
  char c = 'y';
  int n;
  while (c == 'y')
  {
   cout << "Enter number:";
   cin >> n;
   cout << "The factorial of" << n
        << "is" << factorial(n) << '\n';
   cout << "Enter 'y' to continue:";
   cin >> c;
  }
}
```

1.4 Declarations

Variable declarations in C++ consist of a type name followed by one or more variable names. Optionally, declarations may specify default values for variables. Below are some examples of C++ variable declarations.

```
long int i, j, k;
int sum = 0, count = 0;
char c = '\0';
```

Any declaration can be preceded by the keyword `const`. This marks the identifier as being a read-only value. That is, its value may be accessed but not modified.

```
const float pi = 3.1415927;
```

1.5 Operators and Expressions

Table 1.4 presents the most commonly used C++ operators. Many of these are explained in subsequent chapters. The operators are grouped according to precedence, from highest precedence to lowest precedence. Unary and assignment operators are right associative, while all others are left associative.

TABLE 1.4

C++ Operators (highest precedence to lowest precedence)

`++, --, !, ~`	Increment, decrement, logical not, bitwise not
`(type)`	Type cast
`*, /, %`	Multiplication, division, remainder
`+, -`	Addition, subtraction
`<<, >>`	Bit-shift left, Bit-shift right
`<, <=, >, >=`	Relational operators
= =, !=	Equals, not equals
&	Bitwise and
^	Bitwise xor
		Bitwise or
&&	Logical and
||	Logical or
=	Assignment

The logical operators result in a value of zero for false and one for true. Evaluation of logical expressions stops as soon as the result of the expression can be determined. For example, given the expression *(expr1) && (expr2) && (expr3),* if *expr1* is false, then *expr2* and *expr3* are not evaluated. Since *expr1* is false, the entire expression will be false regardless of the values of *expr2* and *expr3*. Similarly, if *expr1* was true and *expr2* was false, *expr3* would not be evaluated. Expressions involving logical OR are evaluated until a true expression is encountered.

The operators ++ and -- combine both assignment and arithmetic. The expression `++i` is equivalent to the assignment statement `i=i+1`, and `--i` is equivalent to `i=i-1`. (This is not necessarily true if `i` and `j` are pointer variables, as discussed in Chapter 4.) Consequently, these operators can be used only with variables. That is, the statement `++(a+b)` is illegal.

Furthermore, these operators have different semantics depending upon whether they appear to the left or right of a variable. The distinction is illustrated as follows.

```
i = 10;
j = ++i + 5 // j is 16 and i is 11
i = 10;
j = i++ + 5; // j is 15 and i is 11
```

In the first sequence, because the increment operator appears to the left of `i`, it performs a pre-increment. In the second example, it appears to the right and therefore performs a post-increment. That is, in the first example, `i` is incremented before the addition; in the second, it is incremented after the addition.

Assignment in C++ is treated no differently than other operators. It may therefore appear anywhere within an expression, as illustrated below.

```
float x,y;
int i = 10, j = 3;
y = (x = i) / j; // x is now 10, y is 3.333
float x, y;
int i = 10, j = 3;
y = x = i / j; // x and y are both 3
```

Also, because the operator is right associative, assignment statements with multiple targets such as $x = y = z = 10.0$ are acceptable.

In addition to the = assignment operator, C++ also defines a set of operators that combine arithmetic and assignment. For example, the statement `i*=j` is equivalent to `i=i*j`. In general, the expression `i` *op*`=j` is equivalent to `i=i` *op* `j` where *op* is an arithmetic, logical, or bit-wise operator.

1.6 Type Conversion

C++ does a great deal of automatic type conversion in expressions and assignment statements. When expressions involve a mixture of `long` and `short` variables (or `float` and `double`), C++ will convert all operands to the longer type and perform the specified operation. When expressions include both integers and reals, C++ converts the integers to reals and performs the operation. When the division operator is used on two integers, the quotient is truncated and the result is an integer. This can cause some unintended results, as illustrated by the sequence below.

```
float x;
int i = 10, j = 3;
x = i / j;
```

Because `i` and `j` are both integers, integer division is performed and `x` is assigned the value 3, not 3.33333 as one might expect.

Character values may also be intermixed with reals and integers. In these cases, the integer value of the character is its ASCII value.

Shorter values may be assigned to longer variables with no side effects. `long` values may also be assigned to `short` variables, but doing so may result in a corrupted value since the high order bits of the `long` value are lost. `Real` values are truncated when assigned to integer variables. The effect of assigning `double` values to `float` variables is machine dependent. Usually, they will be rounded or truncated.

Type conversion can be made explicit through the use of a *type cast.* A type cast has the form *(type) expression* and indicates that the expression is to be converted into the specified type. Type casting can be used to avert the problem identified earlier.

```
float x;
int i = 10, j = 3;
x = (float) i / (float) j;
```

In this example, `i` and `j` are explicitly converted to type `float` and floating point division is therefore performed. Because implicit type conversion can have unintended side effects, it is recommended that programmers use explicit type casting whenever type conversion must occur.

1.7 Standard Input and Output

Unfortunately, a complete understanding of C++ I/O cannot be reached until one has first grasped the concepts of objects and software libraries. Therefore a thorough discussion of this topic is left for a later chapter. In order to use I/O in subsequent examples, however, the syntax is introduced here.

To read a series of values from standard input into a series of variables, one uses a statement of the form:

```
cin >> var1 >> var2 >> var3 ...;
```

Variables are assigned values in order as they are encountered on the standard input device. White space (blanks, tabs, and newlines) is skipped. The list of values read is called an input "stream."

Similarly, to write a series of values to standard output, one uses a statement of the form:

```
cout << val1 << val2 << val3 ...;
```

Note that new lines are not generated unless explicitly included in this output stream:

```
cout << "The result is: " << result << '\n';
```

To provide access to these facilities, a program must contain the statement `#include <iostream.h>`, usually placed at the top of a source file.

Problem Solving Example:

Answer these questions with reference to the numbered statements in the following program.

a. What type of value is stored in z (line 1)?
b. What value is stored in d at line 4?
c. What value is stored in x at line 5?
d. What value is stored in i at line 6?
e. What value is stored in i at line 7?
f. What value is stored in i at line 8?
g. What value is stored in i at line 10?
h. What value is stored in x at line 11?

```
void main()
{
  short z;
  int i = 5;
  int j = 2;
  double d = i/j;
  float x = d;
  i = ++j + 3;
  i = j++ + 4;
  i = ++i - 2;
  char c = ' ';
  i = c;
  x = c;
}
```

A

a. Integer is the default type, so z is a short integer.

b. Since i and j are both integers, integer division is performed. This yields 2 since integer division truncates rather than rounds, which is then converted to 2.0 because d is a double precision floating point.

c. The results of this operation are machine dependent and cannot be predicted.

d. Since j is 2, ++j is 3, so i is 6. Note that the ++ operation changes the value of j just as an assignment statement would.

e. j is 3 (from previous statement), so j++ is 4 and i is 7.

f. i is 7 (from the previous statement) so ++i is 8 and i becomes 6.

g. Since characters are really just short integers, i becomes 32 (the ASCII value for a blank).

h. Treated as an integer, c is 32, so x is 32.0.

CHAPTER 2

Control Structures

2.1 Selectional Structures

2.1.1 The `if` statement

The most general form of the `if` statement is:

```
if (expression)
{
  statement;
  statement;
  ...
}
else
{
  statement;
  statement;
  ...
}
```

If only one statement appears in one of the branches, then the braces are not required, as illustrated in the following example.

```
    if (expression)
      statement;
```

```
else
  statement;
```

The expression to be tested must be enclosed in parentheses. The `else` portion is optional. Grouping symbols in the `if` and the `else` are not required if only one statement is to be selected.

Because C++ has no Boolean data type, any legitimate C++ expression, including assignments and I/O, may be the subject of an `if` statement. Whatever expression is specified is evaluated and, if non-zero, the "true" branch of the `if` is executed. If the expression results in a value of zero, the "false" branch is executed.

This open-ended nature of the `if` is a frequent cause of error for beginning C++ programmers, as shown in the examples below.

```
if (a = 10)// SERIOUS BUG!
{
  ...
}

if ((a > b) & (c < d))// SERIOUS BUG!
{
...
}

if (! a > b)// SERIOUS BUG!
{
...
}
```

In the first example, the programmer has intended to test if `a` is equal to `10`. Instead, the code assigns `10` to `a` then executes the body of the `if`. The `if` body will always be executed because `10` is non-zero. The correct expression would be `if(a==10)`. In the second example, a logical AND was intended but instead a bitwise AND is performed on the results of the expressions `(a>b)` and `(c<d)`. The test expression should instead be `if((a>b)&&(c<d))`. Finally, in the third example, since the NOT operator has a higher precedence than the greater than operator, the expression first performs logical NOT on `a`, then compares the result to `b`. Corrected, this expression should be `if(!(a>b))`.

2.1.2 Conditional Assignment

C++ allows statements of the form *if (test) var = val1 else var = val2* to be written using the notation *var = test ? val1 : val2*. For example, the statement:

```
a = (n > 10) ? b : c;
```

is equivalent to the statement:

```
if (n > 10)
  a = b;
else
  a = c;
```

2.1.3 The `switch` statement

The `switch` statement is used to select statements based on the value of a variable. In the example provided below, the first group of statements is executed if *expression* is equal to *value1*, the second group if *expression* is either *value2* or *value3*, and the third group is selected if none of the other cases apply. The `break` statement transfers control out of the `switch`.

```
switch (expression)
{
 case value1 : statement;
               statement;
               ...
               break;
 case value2 :
 case value3 : statement;
               statement;
               ...
               break;
 default : statement;
           statement;
}
```

When a switch statement is encountered, the specified expression is evaluated and an appropriate case selected. Execution begins at that point and continues downward until either a `break` is executed or the end of the `switch` is reached.

2.2 Looping Constructs

2.2.1 The `while` statement

The two logic controlled loops in C++ are illustrated below.

```
while (expression)
{
  statement;
  ...
}
do
{
  statement;
  ...
} while
(expression);
```

2.2.2 The `for` statement

The other looping construct in C++ is the `for` loop.

```
for (initial expression;
     test expression;
     increment expression)
{
  statement;
  statement;
  ...
}
```

The initial expression is evaluated once, upon entering the loop. The loop continues execution as long as the test expression is true (non-zero). After each loop iteration (essentially, as the last statement of the loop body) the increment is performed. A standard count loop that iterates from 1 to 10 can therefore be implemented as:

```
for (i = 1; i <= 10; ++i)
{
do {}
}
```

Since any legitimate C++ expression may be used in any of the three positions of the `for` statement, this construct is considerably more general than those provided by most other languages.

2.2.3 The `break` and `continue` statements

The `break` statement may be used to terminate a loop at any point. It transfers control to the first statement after the loop. The `continue` statement causes the loop to skip to its next iteration, essentially transferring control to the `while`, do, or `for` statement.

Problem Solving Examples:

Write a C++ program that prints a multiplication table for 1 through 10. Output should be a matrix, like that shown below. Use `for` loops.

1 2 3 4 5 6 7 8 9 10

2 4 6 8 10 12 14 16 18 20

3 6 9 ... and so forth

```
#include <iostream.h>
void main()
{
  int i;
  int j;
  for (i=1; i <= 10; ++i)
 {
   for (j = 1; j <= 10; ++j)
  {
    cout << i*j << "\t";
```

```
      }
       cout << '\n';
     }
   }
```

The output should look like this:

```
 1   2   3   4   5   6   7   8   9   10
 2   4   6   8  10  12  14  16  18   20
 3   6   9  12  15  18  21  24  27   30
 4   8  12  16  20  24  28  32  36   40
 5  10  15  20  25  30  35  40  45   50
 6  12  18  24  30  36  42  48  54   60
 7  14  21  28  35  42  49  56  63   70
 8  16  24  32  40  48  56  64  72   80
 9  18  27  36  45  54  63  72  81   90
10  20  30  40  50  60  70  80  90  100
```

Write a program that converts between kilograms and pounds and between kilometers and miles. One pound is 0.45 kilograms and one kilometer is 0.62 miles. When run, the program presents a menu, like the one below, in a loop until the user selects "Quit". When the user selects an option other than quit, he is prompted for the appropriate data and given the resulting answer. Use a `switch` statement in your program.

1) Convert miles to kilometers
2) Convert kilometers to miles
3) Convert pounds to kilograms
4) Convert kilograms to pounds
5) Quit

```
#include <iostream.h>
void print_menu()
{
 cout << "1) Convert miles to kilometers\n";
```

```
 cout << "2) Convert kilometers to miles\n";
 cout << "3) Convert pounds to kilograms\n";
 cout << "4) Convert kilograms to pounds\n";
 cout << "5) Quit\n\n";
 cout << "Selection:";
}

void main()
{
 int selection;
 float from, to;
 print_menu();
 cin >> selection;
 while (selection !=5)
 {
  switch (selection)
  {
   case 1:
    cout << "Enter miles:";
    cin >> from;
    to = from / 0.62;
    cout << "In kilometers that is:";
    break;
   case 2:
    cout << "Enter kilometers:";
    cin >> from;
    to = from * 0.62;
    cout << "In miles that is:";
    break;
   case 3:
    cout << "Enter pounds:";
    cin >> from;
```

```
    to = from * 0.45;
    cout << "In kilograms that is:";
    break;
   case 4:
    cout << "Enter kilograms:";
    cin >> from;
    to = from / 0.45;
    cout << "In pounds that is:";
    break;
  }
  cout << to << '\n';
  print_menu();
  cin>>selection;
 }
}
```

CHAPTER 3

Non-Primitive Data Types

3.1 Enumerated Types

Enumerated types are defined as illustrated below.

```
enum weekday {Monday, Tuesday, Wednesday, Thursday,
Friday};
```

The values listed within the braces are called enumeration constants and are given integer values starting at zero. Variables of type `enum` may therefore appear anywhere integers may appear. However, some compilers will not allow integers to be directly assigned to enumerated types. Thus, the following is a potential compilation error.

```
weekday d;
int i = 3;
d = i; //not allowed by some compilers!
```

Should one wish to do this, a type cast should be performed as illustrated below.

```
weekday d;
int i = 3;
d = (weekday) i;
```

The effect is to assign d the enumerated constant wednesday. Since most C++ implementations will not provide range checking unless specifically told to do so, programmers should be careful to avoid sequences such as:

```
int i = 10;
...
d = (weekday) i; // executable but bugged
```

Problem Solving Example:

Answer these questions with reference to the numbered statements in the program below.

a. What is the value of p1 at line 2?
b. What is the value of i at line 3?
c. Which statements are potentially bugged?

```
     enum Country {England, France, Germany, Japan};
     enum Pet {Dog, Cat, Hamster};
     void main()
     {
1.    Country c1 = France;
2.    Pet p1 = (Pet) c1;
3.    int i = p1;
4.    Country c2, c3;
5.    Pet p2;
      //... some code ...
6.    c2 = (Country) p2;
7.    p2 = (Pet) c3;
     }
```

a. Cat
b. 3

c. Since Country values range from 0 to 3 and Pet values from 0 to 2, statement 7 would be incorrect if at run time c3 was equal to Japan.

3.2 Arrays

An array definition and initialization are illustrated below.

```
int a[5] = {2,3,5,7,11};
```

This declares `a` to be an array of five integers and initializes it to contain the first five prime numbers. Array indices in C++ are numbered starting at zero and not at one. Thus, `a[0]` and `a[4]` are acceptable references, but `a[5]` does not exist. Again, range checking is usually not provided by default.

The language does not support multidimensional arrays in the traditional sense. However, defining arrays of arrays has the same effect. Thus, one might define a matrix as:

```
float matrix[100][100];
```

The notation `matrix[1][10]` refers to the element at row 1 column 10.

Arrays cannot be copied using the assignment operator. Thus, the following code sequence is illegal.

```
int a[5], b[5];
...
a = b; // ILLEGAL!
```

Problem Solving Example:

Q Write a program that reads in up to 100 positive floating point values, computes their average, then writes out the values and their distance from the average. Assume that the end of the input values is indicated by –1.0.

A In writing this program, be sure to remember that C++ arrays always start at index zero. Set your input counter and `for` loop index appropriately.

```
#include <iostream.h>
```

```
void main()
{
 float a[100];
 int last = -1;
 float sum = 0, n, avg;
 int i;
 cin >> n;
 while (n != -1)
 {
  ++last;
  a[last] = n;
  sum += n;
  cin >> n;
 }
 avg = sum / (float) (last +1);
 for (i = 0; i <= last; ++i)
 {
  cout << a[i] << '\t' << a[i] - avg << '\n';
 }
}
```

3.3 Structures

Structures in C++ are the equivalent of what are called "records" in some other languages. They represent aggregations of related data items. Their declaration and initialization are illustrated as follows.

```
struct student_record {
 int id;
 char classification;
 float gpa;
};
student_record r = {1012, 'J', 3.25};
```

The components of a record are referenced using the '.' operator. Thus, one could say `r.id` or `r.gpa`, for example.

Structure variables may be used with the assignment operator. Thus, one may write:

```
student_record r = {1012, 'J', 3.25}, s;
...
s = r;
...
```

3.4 Unions

A `union` is a `struct` in which all fields begin at the same memory address. A `union` occupies sufficient memory to store its largest field. Unions allow a single storage location to store values of different types, as illustrated below.

```
union union_example {
 int integer_value;
 float float_value;
};
void main()
{
 union_example u;
 u.integer_value = 12;
 cout << u.float_value;
}
```

Since `u.integer_value` and `u.float_value` occupy the same storage, the example stores the bit pattern for 12 in u then writes out whatever floating-point number that bit pattern represents. A reference to `u.integer_value` interprets the value stored at u as an integer, while a reference to `u.float_value` interprets the value as a float.

`Unions` are a potentially unsafe construct but can be convenient when used as fields within a structure, as shown in the following example. In this example, a union is used to declare an array of grades each of which can be either a letter grade or a numerical score.

```
union grade_value {
 float score;
 char letter;
};
enum grade_type {letter_grade, numerical_grade};
struct result_record {
 grade_type type;
 grade_value value;
};
void main()
{
 result_record results[25];
 results[1].type = letter_grade;
 results[1].value = 'A';
 ...
 results[20].type = numerical_grade;
 results[20].value = 85;
 ...
}
```

3.5 The `typedef` Statement

The `typedef` statement is used to create new type identifiers.

```
typedef float Temperature;
typedef char String32[32];
typedef float Matrix[100][100];
```

The `typedef` statement consists of the key word `typedef` followed by an ordinary declaration statement. Subsequent to the sample statements, writing `Temperature t` is equivalent to writing `float t`, writing `String32 s` is equivalent to writing `char s[32]` and writing `Matrix m` is equivalent to writing `float m[100][100]`.

Problem Solving Examples:

Write a set of C++ type definitions for storing information about grades for the students in a class. Store the number of students in the class and the following information for each student:

1. Name (32 characters long)
2. Number of exam grades
3. Exam grades
4. Final exam grade
5. Number of laboratory assignments
6. Laboratory grades

Assume there will be no more than 100 students in a class, no more than 5 exams, and 10 laboratory assignments. Use `typedef`, as appropriate, to make the code easy to read.

```
typedef float LabArray[10];
typedef float ExamArray[5];
typedef char NameString[32];

struct StudentRecord {
 NameString name;
 LabArray labs;
 ExamArray exams;
 float finalExamGrade;
 int numberOfLabs;
 int numberOfExams;
};

typedef StudentRecord StudentArray[100];

struct ClassRecord {
 StudentArray students;
 int numberOfStudents;
};
```

Given the type definitions from the answer to the previous question, write the C++ statements necessary to compute a class's average score on the first exam.

```
ClassRecord r;
int i;
float sum;
for (i = 0; i < r.numberOfStudents; ++i)
{
 sum += r.students[i].exams[0];
}
float avg = sum/r.numberOfStudents;
```

CHAPTER 4
Pointer and Reference Types

4.1 Pointer Variables

A "pointer" variable is one that contains the address of a storage location. The * operator is used to declare that a variable is a pointer. For example, the declaration `int *p` means that `p` will be a pointer to (i.e., contain the address of) a location at which an integer is stored. Alternately, one can declare several pointers to integers with the statement `int *p,*q,*r,*s`. Once a pointer variable `p` has been assigned a value (i.e., made to point to something) the identifier `*p` is used to reference the location to which `p` points. Accessing `*p` is called "dereferencing" the pointer.

One way to assign a pointer variable a value (which should be an address) is to use the & operator, which returns the address of its operand. This is illustrated in the following example.

```
int *p, i = 15;
p = &i;              //p contains the address of I
*p = 20;             //put 20 in memory at address
                     //stored in p (this will be
                     //I)
cout << i;           //writing i writes 20
```

In this example, both `*p` and `i` refer to the same storage cell. This situation, in which a storage location can be referred to by more than one identifier, is called "aliasing."

Pointer variables can also be given values by assigning to them the results of a `new` operation. The `new` operator allocates a storage unit for a specified type and returns the address of the allocated unit. Thus, the statement `p = new int` allocates storage for an integer and puts its address in `p`. If there is insufficient storage to allocate a variable of the specified type, `new` returns a value of zero.

The reverse of `new` is `delete`. The `delete` operator is used to deallocate storage allocated by `new`. The statement `delete p` means "return the storage unit whose address is in `p` to the pool of available storage units."

Pointer variables which have not yet been made to point to something should be assigned the value 0. It is traditional to use a symbolic constant called `NULL` to represent this value. Thus, sequences such as the following are frequently seen.

```
#define NULL 0
...
void main()
{
 int *p = NULL, *q = NULL;
 ...
 if (p == NULL) p = new int;
 ...
}
```

Pointer variables can be made the subject of arithmetic operations. When used with pointer variables, the increment and decrement operators are indexed according to the size of the data type they point to. That is, the expression `++p` is equivalent to `p = p + s`, where `s` is the size of the data type pointed to by `p`. Pointer arithmetic is considered archaic in C++ and is not recommended.

The -> operator is used to reference the individual fields of a structure that are referenced by a pointer. The expression `p->f` is equivalent to `(*p).f`. The use of pointers with structures is illustrated below.

```
student_record *p;
p = new student_record;
p->id = 1013;
p->classification = 'F';
...
delete p;
```

Problem Solving Examples:

Which of the statements in the program below would not compile?

```
void main()
{
1.      int i = 5;
2.      int *p, *q;
3.      p = q;
4.      *p = q;
5.      p = i;
6.      q = &i;
}
```

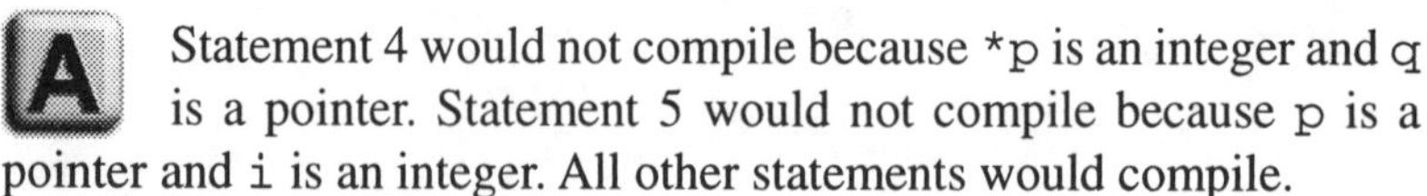

Statement 4 would not compile because `*p` is an integer and `q` is a pointer. Statement 5 would not compile because `p` is a pointer and `i` is an integer. All other statements would compile.

Answer these questions with reference to the numbered statements in the following program.

a. What is the value of `*q` after statement 3 executes?
b. What is the value of `*p` after statement 5 executes?
c. What is the value of `i` after statement 6 executes?
d. What is the value of `*q` after statement 6 executes?

```
void main()
{
1.      int i = 5;
2.      int *p, *q;
3.      q = &i;
4.      p = q;
5.      i = i + 5;
6.      *p = *p + 3;
}
```

a. Statement 3 makes `q` "point to" `i`, so `*q` is another name for `i`. Therefore, the value of `*q` is 5.
b. Statement 4 copies `q` into `p`. Since `q` points to `i`, this makes `p` also point to `i`. Thus, the variable `i` can be referenced three ways: `i`, `*p`, and `*q`. Statement 5 changes `i` to 10, so `*p` is another name for `i`, `*p` is also 10.
c. `*p` and `i` are equivalent, so changing `*p` also changes `i`. `i` is therefore 13.
d. `*q` is also equivalent to `i`, so `*q` is also 13.

4.2 Dynamic Arrays

Pointers can be used to implement arrays whose size is not known until run time. These are known as dynamically allocated arrays. The following method illustrates this.

```
int *a, size;
cout << "how many data points are there?";
cin >> size;
a = new int[size];
for (int i = 0; i < size; ++i)
  cin >> a[i];
delete[] a;
```

The subscript `[]` operator can be used to index any pointer variable. Given that `p` is a pointer, the expression `p[n]` returns the value at address `p+n*s`, where `s` is the size of the data type pointed to by `p`.

Problem Solving Example:

Q Write a program that first reads in the number of values to follow, then reads a list of that number of floating point values, computes their average, then writes out the values and their distance from the average.

```
#include <iostream.h>

void main()
{
 float *a;
 int size;
 float sum = 0, avg;
 int i;
 cin >> size;
 a = new float[size];
 for (i = 0; i < size; ++i)
 {
  cin >> a[i];
  sum = sum + a[i];
 }
 avg = sum / (float) size;
 for(i = 0;i < size; ++i)
 {
  cout << a[i] << '\t' (a[i] - avg) << '\n';
 }
 delete[] a;
}
```

4.3 Reference Variables

Like pointers, reference variables contain the address of a memory cell. Reference variables are declared as *type& var1 = var2*. They must be given an initial value when declared and the value must be something which has an address, not a constant or an expression. The effect of the declaration is to make *var1* an alias for *var2*. The association between a reference variable and the variable it aliases cannot be changed. The example below illustrates the workings of reference variables.

```
int i = 15, j = 50;
int& p = i; //p is an alias for i
p = 20;     //really sets i to 20
cout << i;  //print 20
```

One cannot create arrays of references, nor pointers to references.

4.4 Recursive Structures

A recursive data type is one which makes a reference to itself. For example, a linked list is a recursive data structure since each element of the list contains a pointer to the next element in the list. The example below illustrates how to define a linked list of character values in C++.

```
struct ListCell {
  char contents;
 ListCell *next;
};
```

Problem Solving Example:

Write a program that reads a list of positive integer point values terminated by a –1, then prints the list in reverse order.

```
#include <iostream.h>

struct ListCell;
struct ListCell {
  int value;
  ListCell *next;
};

void main()
{
```

```
  int n;
  ListCell *p = 0;
  ListCell *temp;
  cin>>n;
  while (n != -1)
  {
    temp = new ListCell;
    temp->value = n;
    temp->next = p;
    p = temp;
    cin >> n;
  }
  while (p != 0)
  {
    cout << p->value << '\n';
    temp = p;
    p = p->next;
    delete temp;
  }
}
```

CHAPTER 5

Functions

5.1 Function Structure

A typical C++ function definition is shown below.

```
int power(int base, int exponent)

{

   int product = 1;
  for (int i = 1; i <= exponent; ++i)
   product = product * base;
  return product;
}
```

A function may contain any number of `return` statements. A function terminates with the value specified as soon as any `return` is encountered. Local variables may be declared anywhere within the function, provided they are declared before they are referenced.

C++ does not make a distinction between "procedures" and "functions." All subroutines in C++ are considered functions. However, procedures may be emulated by declaring a function to be of type `void`. Such functions need not include `return` statements. Functions for which no type is specified (not even `void`) are considered to be of type `int`.

Functions that do not have parameters may be specified using either the notation `type f()` or `type f(void)`. When parameterless functions are called, the notation `f()` must be specified.

5.2 Parameter Passing Mechanisms

C++ provides two fundamental mechanisms for passing parameters to functions: pass by value and pass by reference. With the exception of array parameters, which are discussed later, pass by value is the default mechanism. When this mechanism is used, the parameter values in the function call ("actual parameters") are copied into the parameters declared in the function definition ("formal parameters"). Modifying a formal parameter passed by value has no effect on its corresponding actual parameter.

When the pass by reference method is used, a formal parameter becomes an alias for its corresponding actual parameter. Changes made to the formal parameter are immediately reflected in the actual parameter. The `&` symbol is used to indicate that a parameter should be implemented using the reference method.

The overhead involved in copying values from actual to formal parameters can make the pass by value method inappropriate for structures. Consequently, many programmers prefer to pass structures (and objects, as seen later) by reference and pass scalars (integers, reals, and so forth) by value.

Both types of parameters may be prefaced with the keyword `const` to indicate that they are read only parameters. Such parameters can have their values accessed, but cannot be assigned to.

When arrays are used as actual parameters, the corresponding formal parameter is treated as a pointer to the first element of the array. This is illustrated in the following example.

```
#include <iostream.h>
void read_array(int *a, int& size)
{
 cout << "How many data points?";
 cin >> size;
```

```
}

int sum(const int *a, const int size)
{
 int temp = 0;
 for (int I = 0; I < size; ++I)
  temp = temp + a[i];
 return temp;
}

void main()
{
 int data[100], n;
 read_array(data, n);
 cout << "Sum is:" << sum(data,n);
}
```

One could write `int a[]` in place of `int* a` in the two function definitions. The effect is the same. While the former is more readable, the latter has been used to more clearly indicate the semantics of array parameter passing. The `const` qualification of the parameters in `sum()` is not necessary for correctness, but since both parameters are used in a read-only manner they have been so marked.

5.3 Function Return Types

A function may return a value of any type including structured types, pointers, and references. Examples of the former two types are shown in this example.

```
student_record read_record_method1()
// return a student record
{
 student_record r;
 cin >> r.id >> r.classification >> r.gpa;
 return r;
}
```

```
student_record *read_record_method2()
// return a pointer to a student record
{
  student_record *r;
  r = new student_record;
  cin >> r->id >> r->classification
    >> r->gpa;
  return r;
}
void main()
{
 student_record test1, *test2;
 test1 = read_record_method1();
 test2 = read_record_method2();
 cout << test1.id << test2->id;
}
```

Functions that return reference types should not be thought of as returning values but as aliases for storage locations. The function call becomes an alias for the storage location returned by the function. In the example below, the `max()` function returns an alias for the larger of its two parameters.

```
int& max(int& a, int& b)
{
  if (a > b)
    return a;
  else
    return b;
}

void main()
{
```

```
  int q = 5, r = 10, s = 15, t = 20;
  ++max(q,r);                //increments r
  max(s,t) = 3;    //t = 3
  int x = max(q,s)           //x = 15
}
```

Problem Solving Example:

The state of Corusda taxes income (after deducting charitable contributions) according to the scale below.

Income	Tax
up to \$10,000	5%
> \$10,000 and <= \$30,000	10%
> \$30,000 and <= \$70,000	20%
> \$70,000	25%

Write a C++ program that computes the income tax of a user. Implement the program using the functions below.

`GetIncome()`
Prompts the user for income and returns it to the calling routine.

`DeductCharity()`
Given the income, prompts the user for the amount of charitable contributions and deducts this from the income.

`ComputeTax()`
Given income after deductions, computes the amount of tax owed.

`PrintTaxBill()`
Prints amount of tax owed.

```
#include <iostream.h>

float GetIncome()
{
  float income;
  cout << "Enter your income:";
```

```
 cin >> income;
 return income;
}

void DeductCharity(float& income)
{
 float charity;
 cout << "Enter your charitable contributions:";
 cin >> charity;
 income = income - charity;
}

float ComputeTax(float income)
{
 if (income > 70000)
  return income*0.25;
 else if (income > 30000)
  return income*0.2;
 else if (income > 10000)
  return income*0.1;
 else
  return income*0.05;
}

void PrintTaxBill(float tax)
{
 cout << "Your tax bill is: " << tax;
}

void main()
{
 float income = GetIncome();
 DeductCharity(income);
 float tax = ComputeTax(income);
 PrintTaxBill(tax);
}
```

5.4 Function Prototypes

A function prototype specifies the name of a function and the type and number of its parameters, as illustrated below.

```
int power(int, int);
```

Function prototypes allow a programmer to reference a function before its implementation is specified. They also allow sets of related function definitions to be grouped into "header" files, as discussed in the next chapter.

5.5 Optional Parameters

C++ allows function parameters to be given default values, essentially making them optional parameters. The technique is illustrated below.

```
int volume(int width,
           int length = 2,
           int height = 1)
{
  return width*length*height;
}

void main()
{
  int test;
  test = volume(3,2,2); // test is 12
  test = volume(3,2);     // test is 6
  test = volume(2); // test is 4
  . . .
}
```

Since no value was specified for height in the second call to `volume()`, it was assigned a default value of 1, and in the third call to `volume()` both length and height were assigned their default values.

Once a formal parameter is specified as having a default value, all subsequent formal parameters must also be given default values. Thus, the function

```
int volume(int width, int length = 2,
           int height) // NOT ALLOWED!
{
  return width*length*height;
}
```

is not permissible. Similarly, it is not possible to leave "holes" in either the formal or actual parameter lists. Therefore, it would not be possible to call `volume()` specifying only `width` and `height`.

Default parameter values for a function can be specified only once. They cannot be specified both in a function's prototype and its implementation. If function prototypes are used, it is recommended that default parameters be specified there, as illustrated below.

```
//specify defaults in prototype
int volume(int, int = 2, int = 1);

// do not specify them here
int volume(int width, int length, int height)
{
  return width*length*height;
}
```

5.6 Overloaded Functions

It is possible in C++ to define several functions with identical names, provided that they differ in their return types or their formal parameter lists. This is illustrated below.

```
struct fraction {
  int numerator, denominator;
};
void write(int a[], int size)
```

```
{
  for (int i = 0; i <= size-1; ++i)
    cout << a[i] << '\n';
}

void write(char a[], int size)
{
  for (int i = 0; i <= size-1; ++i)
    cout << a[i] << '\n';
}

void write(fraction f)
{
  cout << f.numerator << '/'
    << f.denominator;
}
```

The compiler is able to decipher any call to `write()` by checking the types of the actual parameters.

When several definitions are associated with the same name, that name is said to be overloaded. Thus, the example above illustrates function overloading.

5.7 Operator Overloading

One may overload operators as well as functions. In the example below, the multiplication operator is "told" how to multiply two fraction structures.

```
fraction operator *(fraction f1, fraction f2)
{
  fraction result;
  result.numerator = f1.numerator*f2.numerator;
  result.denominator =
     f1.denominator*f2.denominator;
  return result;
}
```

```
void main()
{
  fraction a={2,3}, b={3,5}, c;
  c = a * b; // c is 6/15
  ...
}
```

The first parameter in a binary operator definition is the left operand and the second is the right operand.

One may only overload existing C++ operators. It is not possible to create new operator symbols, and it is not possible to change the associativity and precedence of an operator.

Problem Solving Example:

Q In mathematics, a complex number is a number of the form $a + bi$ where i represents the imaginary square root of –1. A complex number has two parts: a real part, a, and an imaginary part, bi. Some of the arithmetic with complex numbers is defined below.

$(a + bi) + (c + di) = (a + c) + (b + d)i$

$(a + bi)*(c + di) = (ac - bd) + (ad + bc)i$

$(a + bi) - (c + di) = (a - c) + (b - d)i$

Create a C++ `struct` definition for complex numbers and overload the addition, subtraction, and multiplication operators to work with complex numbers.

```
struct Complex {
 float a;
 float b;
};

Complex operator +(Complex left, Complex right)
{
 Complex result;
```

```
    result.a = left.a + right.a;
    result.b = left.b + right.b;
    return result;
   }

   Complex operator -(Complex left, Complex right)
   {
    Complex result;
    result.a = left.a - right.a;
    result.b = left.b - right.b;
    return result;
   }

   Complex operator *(Complex left, Complex right)
   {
    Complex result;
    result.a = (left.a * right.a) -
               (left.b * right.b);
    result.b = (left.a * right.b) +
               (left.b * right.a);
    return result;
   }
```

5.8 Inline Functions

The run-time overhead associated with function calls makes it inefficient to call functions that contain only a few lines of code. This is because the time spent in the function may be significantly less than the time required to pass the parameters, transfer control, return the value of the function, and so forth. Consequently, C++ allows programmers to specify that a function is to be implemented "inline."

When the compiler encounters a call to a function marked as inline, it does not generate a function call but instead substitutes the body of the function in the place of the function call. An inline function definition is shown below.

```
inline int double(int x)
{
 return 2 * x;
}
```

5.9 Controlling Scope and Lifetime

5.9.1 Scope

Scope refers to the range of statements over which a variable can be referenced. Generally, the scope of a variable in C++ proceeds from the point at which it is declared to the end of the program unit (function or file) in which it is declared. Later, it will be shown that the scope of a variable defined within a class structure is more tightly restricted than this.

The scope resolution operator :: can be used to reference variables which would not otherwise be accessible. This is illustrated below.

```
int i;    // variable is accessible from this
          // point onward
...
float fn()
{
  int i;  // References to i within fn refer to
          // this variable. The previously
          // declared i is now "blocked" and can
          // only be accessed by using the ::
          // operator.
  ...
  cout << i;     // Write out value of local i
  cout << ::i;   // Write out value of
                 // externally declared i.
}
```

Problem Solving Example:

What output would be produced by the following program?

```
#include <iostream.h>

int a = 5;
```

```
void sub1(int a)
{
 a = a + 1;
 cout << a << ::a << '\n';
}

void main()
{
 int a = 2;
 sub1(a);
 cout << a << ::a << '\n';
}
```

A The output statement in `sub1()` produces 3 and 5. The output statement in `main()` produces 2 and 5. In both procedures, the identifier a refers to a local value. In `sub1()`, it is the parameter a and in `main()` it is the local variable a. Note that the change made to a in `sub1()` does not affect the actual argument (`main()`'s local a) since the parameter is not a reference parameter.

5.9.2 Lifetime

The lifetime of a variable refers to the time during which storage for the variable has been allocated. Unless otherwise stated, storage for a variable is allocated when that variable's declaration statement is elaborated and deallocated when the unit in which it is declared terminates. Thus, variables declared within functions are newly created every time the function is activated and destroyed when the function terminates. This is not always desirable, however, and can be overridden in C++ by declaring a variable to be `static`.

Storage for a `static` variable is allocated the first time its declaration statement is encountered and is not deallocated until the entire C++ program terminates. For example, the function below displays 1 the first time it is called, 2 the second time, 3 the third time, and so forth. If a were not declared static, it would print 1 each time it was called.

```
void fn()
{
 static int a = 0;
 a = a + 1;
 cout << a;
}
```

Problem Solving Example:

What would be the output of the program below?

```
#include <iostream.h>

void test()
{
 int j = 1;
 static int i = 0;
 i = i + j;
 cout << j << i;
}

void main()
{
 test();
 test();
}
```

The first call to `test()` produces 1 and 1. Because `i` is `static` and `j` is not, in the second call to `test()`, `j` is reinitialized to 1 but `i` retains its previous value of 1. The second call therefore produces 1 and 2.

CHAPTER 6 Preprocessor Directives and Header Files

6.1 The Preprocessor

Before the translation phase of compilation begins, a C++ program is first treated by the C++ preprocessor. The preprocessor performs several tasks, the most significant of which are:

1. Copy specified files into the current source file
2. Perform text substitutions in the source file
3. Select sections of code to be compiled or skipped by the compiler

Instructions to the preprocessor are given through "directives." These are indicated by the # symbol and must not be preceded by white space.

6.2 Header files, `#include`, and Separate Compilation

The `#include <filename>` directive is used to copy a specified file into the file being processed. If the file name is enclosed in angle brackets, the preprocessor will search for the file on the system "include file" search path. If the name is enclosed in double quotes, the preprocessor will search for the file on the user's current directory.

```
#include <iostream.h>
#include "myfile.h"
```

The `#include` directive is most often used to provide programmers access to groups of related type definitions and function prototypes located in "header" files. Header files are traditionally given a file extension of "h" to distinguish them from source code files which are usually given an extension of "cc", "cpp", or "C". C++ installations usually provide a large set of header files defining functions for tasks such as string manipulation, I/O, mathematical computation, and so forth.

Some header files are standard and will be included with every C++ installation. For example, the file `iostream.h` and `string.h` provide I/O and string manipulation functions, respectively. These are discussed in later chapters. Some of the other standard header files are discussed at the end of this chapter, but a complete treatment is beyond the current scope. Programmers should consult their compiler documentation for a description of what has been included in their implementation.

Header files should contain only definitions and function prototypes. Associated with a header file will be a corresponding source code file that contains the complete specification of the functions whose prototypes appear in the header file. To create a C++ executable file, each source code file is compiled separately and the resulting object code files are linked using a system linker. (Usually, the same program that provides compilation can also provide linking.)

6.3 Symbolic Constants

The `#define` directive can be used to define symbolic constants.

```
#define PI 3.1415927
#define MAX_SIZE 100
#define ERROR "An error has occurred."
```

Symbols defined this way are quite different from those defined using the `const` declaration shown in Chapter 1. The former exist only during the preprocessing stage, while the latter are compiled in a way much like variables.

Symbolic constants defined this way instruct the preprocessor to perform text substitution. That is, with reference to the example above, the preprocessor will simply substitute the string "3.1415927" whenever it encounters `PI` in the source file. After preprocessing, the resulting altered text is made the subject of the compiler, which consequently never "sees" `PI`.

6.4 Macros

Macros are another form of text substitution that can be specified using the `#define` directive. A macro is defined with parameters and takes the general form:

```
#define name(arg1, arg2, ...) substitute-text
```

For example, one might define the following:

```
#define sqr(x) (x)*(x)
```

Subsequent to this definition, upon encountering the text `sqr(a)` the preprocessor substitutes `(a)*(a)`, upon encountering `sqr(a+b)` it substitutes `(a+b)*(a+b)`, and so forth. Since the preprocessor performs text substitution only, upon encountering `sqr("Hello world")` it would substitute `("Hello world")*("Hello world")` and proceed with its processing.

The last example illustrates that macros are potentially very unsafe constructs. In fact, they are a holdover from C. Since they provide functionality very similar to that provided by inline functions, there is no reason to use them in C++ and they should be avoided.

6.5 Conditional Compilation

A programmer can cause the preprocessor to select sections of code to be compiled or not compiled by using either the `#ifdef` ("if defined") or `#ifndef` (if not defined) directives. The two have the same form. The `#ifdef` is shown as follows.

```
#ifdef symbol
... some code ...
#else
... some code ...
#endif
```

The code contained within the "if" section of the block is compiled if the specified symbol is known to the preprocessor. If the symbol is not known, the code within the "else" section is compiled. The effect of the `#ifndef` directive is analogous. In either case, the `#else` is optional. Symbols can be defined by statements of the form `#define symbol`.

These directives are very useful if a program must include machine specific sections of code. The technique is illustrated here.

```
#ifdef MS_DOS
  // code specific to MS_DOS
#endif
#ifdef UNIX
 // code specific to UNIX
#endif
```

To compile this code for a specific platform, a programmer might or may include either the line `#define MS_DOS` or `#define UNIX` at the top of the source file. Only the appropriate blocks of code are then compiled.

6.6 Avoiding Duplicate Definitions

Header files and the `#include` directive provide a simple mechanism for creating software libraries but can cause problems since it is easily possible for the same header files to be copied several times into the same source file. The problem is illustrated in the following example.

```
//This is file class.h
#include "student.h"
```

```
struct class_record {
 student_record students[100];
 int enrollment;
}
...
//This is file grade_book.cc
#include "student.h"
#include "class.h"
```

In the example, the definitions in STUDENT.H end up being copied into GRADE_BOOK.CC twice: once as a direct consequence of `#include "student.h"` and indirectly from `#include "class.h"` because CLASS.H also includes STUDENT.H. Compiler errors will be generated for every duplicate definition. Of course, a careful programmer could avoid this problem by not including STUDENT.H in GRADE_BOOK.CC, but for large systems with many different header files it is difficult or impossible to keep an accurate track of which files are included in which other files.

Because of this problem, it is common practice to associate with each header file a preprocessor symbol that serves as a flag to indicate whether or not the contents of that file have been compiled. This technique is illustrated below. In the example, the GRADE_BOOK.CC file may contain more than one copy of STUDENT.H, but the definitions are compiled only the first time they are encountered.

STUDENT.H

```
#ifndef student
#define student
struct student_record {
 int id;
 char classification;
 float gpa;
};
void read_student(student_record&);
#endif //the last statement in the file
```

CLASS.H

```
#ifndef class
#define class
#include "student.h"
struct class_record {
 student_record students[100];
 int enrollment;
}
...
#endif // the last statement in the file
```

GRADEBOOK.CC

```
#include "student.h"
#include "class.h"
void main()
{
 student s;
 class c;
 ...
}
```

Problem Solving Example:

Produce C++ "h" and ".cpp" files for the complex number type defined in the question at the end of Section 5.7.

The file COMPLEX.H looks like this:

```
#ifndef COMPLEX_H
#define COMPLEX_H

struct Complex {
 float a;
 float b;
};
```

```
Complex operator +(Complex left, Complex right);
Complex operator -(Complex left, Complex right);
Complex operator *(Complex left, Complex right);

#endif
```

The file COMPLEX.CPP looks like this:

```
#include "complex.h"

Complex operator +(Complex left, Complex right)
{
 Complex result;
 result.a = left.a + right.a;
 result.b = left.b + right.b;
 return result;
}

Complex operator -(Complex left, Complex right)
{
 Complex result;
 result.a = left.a - right.a;
 result.b = left.b - right.b;
 return result;
}

Complex operator *(Complex left, Complex right)
{
 Complex result;
 result.a = (left.a * right.a) -
       (left.b * right.b);
 result.b = (left.a * right.b) +
       (left.b * right.a);
 return result;
}
```

6.7 Some Useful Library Files

6.7.1 CTYPE.H

The header file CTYPE.H defines several functions for testing character data. In the table below, the specified function is true if the argument is in the specified range.

TABLE 6.1

`int isalnum(int)`	upper or lower case letter or digit
`int islower(int)`	lower case letter
`int isalpha (int)`	upper or lower case letter
`int isprint(int)`	a printing character, 0 x 20 – 0 x 7E
`int isascii(int)`	low order byte range 0 – 127
`int ispunct(int)`	a punctuation character (`isspace()` or `iscntrl()`)
`int iscntrl(int)`	a delete or control character, 0x7F or 0x00 – 0x1F
`int isspace(int)`	space, tab, carriage return, newline, vertical tab, or form feed
`int isdigit(int)`	a digit
`int isupper(int)`	an upper case letter
`int isgraph(int)`	like `isprint()` except the space character is excluded
`int isxdigit(int)`	is a hex digit, 0 – 9 and A – F

In addition to these, the file defines functions `int toupper(int)` and `int tolower(int)`. These convert letters to upper and lower case, respectively. They return an unchanged copy of their argument if it is not a character in the expected range.

6.7.2 ASSERT.H

The header file ASSERT.H defines a macro called `assert` which is used to specify truth conditions at various places in a program. These "assertions" state properties that should be true if the program is operating correctly, as in this example.

```
// return first character in a list
char first(ListCell* List)
{
  assert(List != NULL);
  return List->contents;
}
```

If an assertion is encountered and its specified condition is evaluated as false, the program is terminated and an appropriate error message is displayed. (The particular message is machine dependent, but usually it specifies the function and line where the failed assertion occurred.)

Assertions are extremely useful debugging aids but will increase the size of an object file. Therefore, the macro is designed so that `assert` statements will be compiled only if the symbol NODEBUG is not defined.

6.7.3 MATH.H

The file MATH.H contains functions useful for performing mathematical computations. Some of them are given below. Typically, several variations of each function are defined to operate with different data types. The functions in Table 6.2 accept arguments of type `double`.

TABLE 6.2

`sin(), cos(), tan()`	Trigonometric functions
`asin(), acos(), atan()`	Arc-trigonometric functions
`sinh(), cosh(), tanh()`	Hyperbolic functions
`log(), log10()`	Natural and base-10 logarithms
`exp()`	e to the power of x
`ciel()`	Finds smallest integer not less than x

floor()	Finds largest integer not greater than x
sqrt()	Square root
abs()	Absolute value
pow(base, exponent)	Power (exponentiation)

6.7.4 STDLIB.H

This file contains a miscellaneous group of definitions that are too numerous to list exhaustively. Some of the more frequently used functions are given in Table 6.3.

TABLE 6.3

int atoi(char*s)	Convert a string of characters to an integer
float atof(char*s)	Convert a string of characters to float
int exit(int)	Exit the program and return the specified value
RAND_MAX	A symbol representing the largest random number generated by rand()
NULL	Symbol representing an "empty" pointer
int rand()	Return a pseudo-random integer in the range 0 to RAND_MAX
srand(unsigned int)	Set the seed value used by rand()
double strtod(char*s)	Convert character string to double
long strtol(char*s)	Convert character string to long
unsigned long strtoul(char*s)	Convert character string to unsigned long

The following program illustrates the use of the random number generator. This program simulates the toss of 100 coins. The function `srand()` should be called only once. The `rand()` function produces a pseudo-random sequence of integers based on the seed value. If the program is given the same seed value each time it is run, it produces the same sequence of "random" integers. Therefore, it is common to use the system clock to set the random number seed.

```
#include <iostream.h>
#include <stdlib.h>
#include <time.h>

void main()
{
  int head = 0, tails = 0;
  time_t t = time(NULL);
  srand(t);
  for(int i = 1; i <= 100; ++i)
    if (rand() % 2 == 0)
      ++heads;
    else
      ++tails;
  cout << heads << '\t' << tails;
}
```

Problem Solving Example:

Write a C++ program that generates 1,000 random numbers between 0 and 9 (inclusive) and prints out the number of 0s, ls, 2s, and so forth that were generated.

```
#include <stdlib.h>
#include <time.h>
#include <iostream.h>

void main()
{
  int counts[10];
```

```
    int i, n;
    time_t t = time(NULL);
    srand(t);
    for (i = 0; i <= 9; ++i)
      counts[i] = 0;
    for(i = 1; i <= 1000; ++i)
    {
      n = rand() % 10;
      counts[n] = counts[n] + 1;
    }
    for (i = 0; i <= 9; ++i)
      cout << counts[i] << '\n';
}
```

6.7.5 TIME.H

This file contains a number of functions and definitions that can be used to access the computer system clock. Some of these are given below. Following the table, a program is presented that illustrates the use of the time functions.

TABLE 6.4

`time_t`	A type identifier used to represent time values
`clock_t`	A type identifier used to represent clock values
`CLOCKS_PER_SEC`	A symbolic constant representing the number of processor clock cycles per second

`struct tm {`
`int tm_sec;`
`int tm_min;`
`int tm_hour;`
`int tm_mday;`
`int tm_mon;`
`int tm_year;`
`int tm_wday;`
`int tm_yday;`
	A structure representing the time on a 24–hour clock, day of month (1 to 31), month (0 to 11), weekday (Sunday equals 0), year – 1900, day of year (0 to 365), and a flag that is nonzero if daylight savings time is in effect.

`int tm_isdst;`
`};`
`struct tm*localtime`
`(const time_t*timer);`
	Returns a pointer to the structure containing 24 hour time, given a `time_t`. This structure is a static that is overwritten with each call.

```
#include <time.h>
#include <iostream.h>

void main ()
{
   time_t timer;
   struct tm *tblock;

   // get time in seconds
   timer = time(NULL);


   // create a tm structure
   tblock = localtime(&timer);

   // write out date
   cout << tblock->tm_mon + 1 << "/"
     << tblock->tm_mday << "/"
     << tblock->tm_year + 1900 << "\n";

   clock_t ck = clock();

   //write out seconds elapsed since program
   //execution
   cout << ck / (double)CLOCKS_PER_SEC;
}
```

Problem Solving Example:

Write a C++ function that delays a number of seconds specified as a double.

```
void delay(double d)
{
 double start = clock()/(double)CLOCKS_PER_SEC;
 double seconds = 0.0;
 while (seconds < d)
 {
  seconds = clock() /
          ((double)CLOCKS_PER_SEC) - start;
 }
}
```

CHAPTER 7

Working with Character Strings

7.1 Character Strings

Character strings in C++ are implemented as arrays of characters. Two methods for declaring and initializing a string are illustrated below.

```
char greeting[32] = "Hello World!";
char name[] = "Joan Smith";
```

The first example allocates 32 characters for `greeting` and loads "Hello World" starting at `greeting[0]`. Extra space is unused. The second example allocates to `name` exactly the amount of space required to store the string "Joan Smith."

C++ provides a library of string processing functions in the header file STRING.H. These are summarized in the following tables. Note that calls to the "destructive" string functions result in changes to the string specified as the first argument to the function. Consequently, these cannot be called with a `const` string as the first argument.

TABLE 7.1
Nondestructive String Function Table

`int strcmp(char* s1, char* s2)`	Returns 0 if `s1` is equal to `s2`, `s2`, –1 if `s1` is less than `s2`,and +1 if `s1` is greater than `s2`.
`int strncmp(char* s1, char* s2, int n)`	Compares most `n` chara-cters in `s1` and `s2`
`int strlen(char* s)` `char* strchr(char* s, int c)`	String length Returns pointer to first occurrence of `c` in `s`
`char* strrchr(char* s, int c)`	Returns pointer to last occurrence of `c` in `s`
`char* strpbrk(char* s1, char* s2)`	Returns pointer to first occurrence in `s1` of any of the characters that are in`s2`
`int strspn(char* s1, char* s2)`	Returns the length of the largest prefix of `s1` that consists entirely of charac-ter in `s2`
`int strcspn(char* s1, char* s2)`	Returns the length of the largest prefix of `s1` that consists entirely of charac-ters not in `s2`

TABLE 7.2
Destructive String Function Table

`char* strcpy(char* s1, char* s2)`	Copies `s2` into `s1`
`char* strncpy(char* s1, char* s2, int n)`	Copies at most `n` characters from `s2` into `s1`
`char* strcat(char* s1, char* s2)`	Concatenates `s2` on to the end of `s1`

`char* strncat(char* s1, char* s2, int n)`	Concatenates at most `n` characters from `s2` onto `s1`
`char* strtok(char* s1, char* delim)`	Break `s1` into tokens (See text)

The string library package adopts the convention of using the character '`\0`' to mark the end of a string. This "end of string" marker is automatically inserted and maintained by the library functions, and for most purposes the programmer need not be aware of its existence. However, it may be important to remember that every string will contain this one additional character. Thus, the variable `greeting` can hold at most 31 characters of data.

When comparing strings, characters from the two strings are compared in succession until the characters are not equal or until an end of string ('`\0`') is encountered. Similarly, when copying one string to another, successive characters are copied until the end of string mark in the source string is encountered. Because range checking is usually not the default, caution must be exercised when copying and comparing strings.

The `strtok()` function is used to process the individual "tokens" in a string. A token is a sequence of characters forming a meaningful lexical unit (a word, for example). To use `strtok()`, it should be called once with the first argument being the string to be processed and the second a string indicating the delimeter characters that mark the end of a token. After this call, the function will replace the first occurrence in `s` of a `delim` character with '`\0`' and return a pointer to the first token in `s`. The first time the function is called this will usually be a pointer equal to `s` since a string usually begins with a token.

Subsequent calls to `strtok()` should be made using `NULL` as its first argument. The function will return a pointer to the next token in `s` each time it is called. It will return `NULL` when there are no more tokens in `s`. The following program illustrates the use of `strtok()`.

Also following are a few examples illustrating the workings of some of the other string functions. All functions that return pointers return `NULL` if they are unsuccessful.

```
#include <string.h>
#include <iostream.h>
void main()
{
  char *s = "This is it", *delim =" ", *tok;
// set up strtok for processing s
// and return pointer to first token
  tok = strtok(s, delim);
  do {
   cout << tok << '\n';
// get pointer to the next token, NULL
// if none
   tok = strtok(NULL, delim);
 } while (tok != NULL);
}
```

Problem Solving Examples:

Q Write a C++ function that returns the number of words in a character string. A word is a sequence of non-blank characters followed by a single space. Assume the string starts with a non-blank character. The parameter to the function should not be changed by the function. Use the `strtok()` function.

A

```
int words(char* s)
{
 char* copy = new char[strlen(s)];
 strcpy(copy, s);
 char* delim = " ";
 char* tok = strtok(copy, delim);
 int count = 0;
 while (tok != NULL)
 {
  ++count;
```

```
    tok = strtok(NULL, delim);
  }
  delete [] copy;
  return count;
}
```

Write a C++ function that returns the number of words in a character string. A word is a sequence of lowercase letters. The parameter to the function should not be changed by the function. Use the `strspn()` function.

A

```
int words(char* s)
{
  int count = 0;
  char* letters = "abcdefghijklmnopqrstuvwxyz";
  int start = 0;
  int length;
  do
  {
    length = strspn(&(s[start]), letters);
    if (length != 0)
    {
      count = count + 1;
      start = start + length + 1;
    }
  } while (length != 0 && start <= strlen(s));
  return count;
}
```

CHAPTER 8

Classes and Objects

8.1 Class Definition

Just as a structure definition encapsulates a set of related data items, a class definition encapsulates related data items and functions that manipulate them. A simple class definition for a "vehicle" data type is shown below.

```
class vehicle {
public:
  int wheels;
  float weight;
  void initialize(float in_weight,
                  int in_wheels = 4);
  float wheel_loading();
  void honk();
};
```

The elements defined within a class (wheels, weight, initialize, etc.) are referred to as "members" of the class.

Function class members are called "methods" to distinguish them from "freestanding" functions. Typically, only the method prototypes appear within the class definition. Subsequent to the class definition, the methods would be elaborated as shown on the next page.

```
void vehicle::initialize(float in_weight,
                         int in_wheels = 4)
{
  wheels = in_wheels;
  weight = in_weight;
}
```

The syntax `vehicle::initialize()` specifies that the specific `initialize()` method being implemented is the one included in the `vehicle` class, as opposed to some other `initialize()` method, or an `initialize()` function not associated with any class.

It is traditional to place a class definition in a header file and the implementation of its methods in a corresponding source code file. Following this practice, the vehicle class definition would be present in VEHICLE.H and its implementation in VEHICLE.CC.

It is possible to include a complete method definition within the bounds of a class definition, but doing so automatically marks the function as inline. Consequently, this should be done only for very small (several lines) functions.

The example below shows how the `vehicle` class would be used. The components of a class variable are selected using the '`.`' operator, just as components of a structure are selected. Class variables, such as `s1` and `s2` in the example, are called "objects" in C++. The process of selecting a method from a particular object is often described as sending a *message* to that object. Thus, the statement `s2.honk()` is interpreted as sending `s2` the `honk()` message. Objects therefore receive messages and execute their methods appropriately.

```
main()
{
 vehicle s1, s2;
 s1.initialize(2000);
 cout << s1.wheel_loading();
 s2.initialize(25, 2);
 s2.honk();
 ...
}
```

8.2 The `public`, `private`, and `protected` keywords

`Public` class members are accessible from anywhere, `private` members are accessible only within the class itself—they are not inherited into derived classes—and `protected` members are accessible whithin the class and any of its derived classes. The creation of separate `public`, `private`, and `protected` sections is called *information hiding* and is a fundamental principle of object-oriented programming.

It is convenient to think of a class as defining a set of attributes and behaviors. Methods specify behaviors, while variables (`wheels`, `weight`) specify attributes. Usually, the `public` section of a class is used to define methods only while the variables representing attributes are placed in the `protected` section of a class. Methods are usually provided to set and access class attributes (*accessor methods*). A modified `vehicle` class incorporating these principles is presented below. Since the number of wheels and base weight of a vehicle are presumably unchangeable values, only accessor methods are provided. Inline method definitions are used.

```
class vehicle {
public:
      void initialize(float in_weight,
                           int in_wheels = 4);
      int GetWheels()
         { return wheels; };
      int GetWeight()
         { return weight; };
      float wheel_loading();
      void honk();
protected:
      int wheels;
      float weight;
};
```

8.3 Specialized Methods

8.3.1 Constructor Methods

Because initialization methods are so common, a class definition usually specifies a "constructor" method. Constructor methods are automatically called when an object is declared. They are given the name of the class itself and must not be given a return type specification. Thus, the `initialize ()` method of class vehicle can be replaced with a vehicle constructor method.

```
class vehicle {
public:
  vehicle(float in_weight, int in_wheels = 4)
  {
    weight = in_weight;
    wheels = in_wheels;
  }
  //...rest as before
};
```

Given this definition, statements such as `vehicle v1, v2(2000), v3(25, 2)` could be used to create vehicle objects.

A more concise syntax for constructor methods allows the parameter list of a constructor method to be followed by one or more initialization expressions of the form *variable(value)*. The syntax is illustrated below.

```
class vehicle {
public:
  vehicle(float in_weight, int in_wheels = 4) :
  weight(in_weight),
  wheels(in_wheels)
  {
  }
  //...rest as before
};
```

Since C++ allows for function overloading, classes may provide several constructor methods. In fact, it is recommended that all classes provide a constructor method that takes no parameters. This is referred to as a "default" constructor.

```
class vehicle {
public:
  vehicle()
  {
    weight = 0;
    wheels = 0;
  };
  vehicle(float in_weight, int in_wheels = 4)
  {
    weight = in_weight;
    wheels = in_wheels;
  };
  //...rest as before
};
```

Problem Solving Examples:

Q Recall the definition of complex numbers given in the review question for Section 6.6. Develop a complex number class along with addition, subtraction, and multiplication operations. Provide constructors that allow complex numbers to be constructed in the following ways:

```
Complex c;            //produces 0.0 + 0.0i;
Complex c(3.4);       //produces 3.4 + 0.0i;
Complex c(2.5, 3.4); //produces 2.5 + 3.4i;
```

The file COMPLEX.H looks like this:

```
#ifndef COMPLEX_H
#define COMPLEX_H

class Complex {
 Complex();
 Complex(float inA);
 Complex(float inA, inB);
 Complex operator +(Complex right);
 Complex operator -(Complex right);
 Complex operator *(Complex right);
private:
 float a;
 float b
};

#endif
```

The file COMPLEX.CPP looks like this:

```
#include "complex.h"

Complex::Complex()
{
 a = b = 0.0;
}

Complex::Complex(float inA)
{
 a = inA;
 b = 0.0;
}

Complex::Complex(float inA, float inB)
{
 a = inA;
```

```
 b = inB;
}

Complex Complex::operator +(Complex right)

{
 Complex result;
 result.a = a + right.a;
 result.b = b + right.b;
 return result;
}

Complex Complex::operator -(Complex right)
{
 Complex result;
 result.a = a - right.a;
 result.b = b - right.b;
 return result;
}

Complex Complex::operator *(Complex right)

{
 Complex result;
 result.a = (a * right.a) -
      (b * right.b);
 result.b = (a * right.b) +
      (b * right.a);
 return result;
}
```

Q A *stack* is a collection of values, upon which, two operations called *push* and *pop* may be performed. *Push* adds a value to the "top" of the stack, and *pop* removes the item at the top of the stack. Write C++ ".h" and ".cpp" files that define a class that acts as a stack of up to 100 integers. The following example illustrates a client program for the `stack` class.

```
#include "stack.ccp"
#include <iostream.h>

void main()
{
 Stack s;
 s.Push(13);
 s.Push(7);
 s.Push(23);
 cout << s.Pop(); //writes 23
 cout << s.Pop(); //writes 7
 cout << s.Pop(); //writes 13
 s.Push(45);
 cout << s.Pop(); //writes 45
}
```

A The file STACK.H is:

```
#ifndef STACK_H
#define STACK_H

class Stack {
public:
 Stack();
 void Push(int value);
 int Pop();
protected:
 int contents[100];
 int top;
};

#endif
```

The file STACK.CPP is:

```
#include "stack.h"
```

```
Stack::Stack()
{
 top = -1;
}

void Stack::Push(int value)
{
 ++top;
 contents[top] = value;
}

int Stack::Pop()
{
 int result = contents[top];
 --top;
 return result;
}
```

8.3.2 Destructor Methods

Some data types may require action to be taken when an object of that type is deallocated. These actions can be defined in a "destructor" method. Destructor methods are identified by the class name preceded by the ~ mark. For example, the destructor method for the `vehicle` class would be called `~vehicle`. Destructor methods are needed for classes that contain dynamically allocated data structures such as linked lists or dynamic arrays, but are not truly necessary for other classes. Like constructors, destructor methods should not be given a return type specification.

Problem Solving Example:

Q Modify your `stack` class so that it includes a constructor that allows a client to specify a maximum size for the stack. Also add a destructor method. The example client program would be modified as follows.

```
#include "stack.ccp"
#include <iostream.h>

void main()
{
 Stack s(32); //a stack of up to 32 integers
 //... rest as before.
}
```

A The file STACK.H is:

```
#ifndef STACK_H
#define STACK_H

class Stack {
public:
 Stack(int size);
 ~Stack();
 void Push(int value);
 int Pop();
protected:
 int* contents;
 int top;
 int maxSize;
};

#endif
```

The file STACK.CPP is:

```
#include "stack.h"

Stack::Stack(int size)
{
 contents = new int[size];
 top = -1;
 maxSize = size;
}
```

```
Stack::~Stack()
{
 delete [] contents;
}

//...rest as before
```

8.3.3 Copy Methods

Along with constructors and destructors, it is also common to associate copy methods with class types. (These are called "default copy constructors" by some authors.) Copy method prototypes have the form *type (const type& variable)* and specify how to construct a copy of an object. Copy methods are automatically called when, for example, an object is passed by value into a function. It is particularly important to specify copy constructors for objects that contain dynamically allocated data structures. Return types should not be specified for copy constructors.

Problem Solving Example:

Add a copy constructor to your `stack` class.

The file STACK.H is:

```
#ifndef STACK_H
#define STACK_H

class Stack {
public:
 Stack(int size);
 Stack(Stack& s);
 ~Stack();
 void Push(int value);
 int Pop();
protected:
 int* contents;
```

```
    int top;
    int maxSize;
   };

   #endif
```

The file STACK.CPP is:

```
#include "stack.h"

//as before with the addition of:

Stack::Stack(Stack& s)
{
 contents = new int[s.maxSize];
 top = s.top;
 maxSize = s.maxSize;
 for (int I = 0; I <= s.top; ++I)
 {
  contents[i] = s.contents[i];
 }
}
```

8.3.4 Operator Methods

Many classes will want to provide operator methods. For example, a matrix or complex number class would presumably overload the arithmetic operators. It is customary for all classes, however, to overload the assignment operator. When defined as a method for a given class, the assignment operator has a single parameter which is a reference to an object of that class, copies that object, and then returns a reference to the object being assigned to. The keyword `this` is used within a method definition as a pointer to the object receiving the message (the "host" object). The general form of an assignment operator method is therefore

```
class_type& operator =(const class_type& source)
{
// ... copy source into host object ...
```

```
 return *this //return a reference to the
              //object itself (not a pointer to
              //the object)
}
```

The implementation of an assignment operator method is given in the example below, where the complete definition of the vehicle class is presented.

```
class vehicle {
public:
  //constructor methods
  vehicle()
  {
    weight = 0;
    wheels = 0;
  }

  vehicle(float in_weight, int in_wheels = 4)
  {
    weight = in_weight;
    wheels = in_wheels;
  }

  //copy constructor
  vehicle(const vehicle& v)
    {wheels = v.wheels; weight = v.weight; }

  //operator definitions
  vehicle& operator =(const vehicle& v)
  {
    wheels = v.wheels;
    weight = v.weight;
    return *this;
  }
```

```
  //accessor methods
   int GetWheels() { return wheels; }
   int GetWeight() { return weight; }

//other methods
   float wheel_loading()
     { return (weight / wheels); }
   void honk() { cout << "Beep Beep!\n"; }

//destructor method (no action required
//because no dynamic memory)
  ~vehicle() { }
protected:
  int wheels;
  float weight;
};
```

Problem Solving Example:

Overload the assignment operator for your `stack` class.

The file STACK.H is:

```
#ifndef STACK_H
#define STACK_H

class Stack {
public:
 Stack(int size);
 Stack(Stack& s);
 ~Stack();
 Stack& operator =(Stack& s);
 void Push(int value);
```

```
  int Pop();
protected:
  int* contents;
  int top;
  int maxSize;
};

#endif
```

The file STACK.CPP is:

```
//rest as before with the addition of:
Stack& Stack::operator =(Stack& s)

{
 delete [] contents;
 contents = new int[s.maxSize];
 top = s.top;
 maxSize = s.maxSize;
 for (int I = 0; I <= s.top; ++I)
 {
  contents[i] = s.contents[i];
  return *this;
 }
}
```

8.4 `friend` Classes and Functions

Under normal circumstances, the protected members of a class cannot be accessed outside of that class. One way to provide an exception to this is through the `friend` mechanism. When a function or class is defined to be a friend of another class, it has access to all of that class's members. Friendly functions are specified in a class definition by stating `friend` *prototype* and friendly classes by stating `friend` *class_name* anywhere within the class definition. It is usual, however, to place `friend` declarations at the very top of a class definition. The technique of declaring a `friend` function is illustrated in the following example.

```
class vehicle {
  friend void reset(vehicle, int, int);
public:
  //...rest as before
}

void reset(vehicle v, int in_wheels,
           int in_weight)
{
//note access to protected members of vehicle
  v.wheels = in_wheels;
  v.weight = in_weight;
}
```

The `friend` mechanism violates the usual class access mechanism and should be used sparingly. The example provided is not a particularly good use of the mechanism and is provided for pedagogical purposes only.

8.5 A Linked List Class

To tie all the various class definition features together into a single example, a program is presented in which a linked list of characters is defined. Note that pointers are used with objects in the same manner as structures.

The class `ListCell` represents a single node in a list. Each node contains a character value and a pointer to the next node in the list. The class `List` encapsulates a pointer to the first node in a list and various list manipulation functions.

The function `List::Add(char c)` creates a new `ListCell` containing `c` and then sets `First` to point to this new cell. The effect is to insert the new node at the beginning of the list. Note that the `List()` constructor initializes `First` to `NULL`. This ensures that the last node in a list will always have a `Next` value of `NULL`.

```
#include <iostream.h>
#define NULL 0
```

```
class List;
class ListCell {
friend List;
public:
    ListCell(char c, ListCell *p = NULL)
      : contents(c), Next(p) { };
    ListCell()
      : contents('\0'), Next(NULL) {};
    ListCell(const ListCell& lc)
    {
      contents = lc.contents;
      Next = lc.Next;
    };

    ListCell& operator =(const ListCell& lc)
    {
      contents = lc.contents;
      Next = lc.Next; return *this;
    };

    char GetContents() {return contents;};
    ListCell* GetNext(){return Next;};

   ~ListCell() { };
protected:
    char contents;
    ListCell* Next;
};

class List {
public:
  List() {First = NULL;};

  List (const List&);
  List& operator =(List& l);

  void add(char c)
  {
```

```
    First = new ListCell(c, First);
  };

  void remove(char);
  int IsIn(char);

  ~List();
protected:
  ListCell* First;
};

List::List(const List& l)
 {
if (l.First == NULL)
    First = NULL;
else
  {
    First =
     new ListCell(l.First->contents,NULL);
     ListCell *pl = l.First->Next;
     ListCell *p2 = First;
     while (pl != NULL)
     {
        p2->Next =
        new ListCell(pl->contents,
        NULL);
        p2 = p2->Next;
        pl = pl->Next;
     }
  }
 }
List& List::operator =(List& l)
{
  if (l.First == NULL) return *this;
  ListCell *q = First, *next;
  while (q != NULL)
```

```
  {
        next = q->Next;
        delete q;
        q = next;
  }
  First =
    new ListCell(l.First->contents,NULL);
  ListCell *pl = l.First->Next;
  ListCell *p2 = First;
  while (pl != NULL)
  {
    p2->Next =
         new ListCell(pl->contents, NULL);
       p2 = p2->Next;
    pl = pl->Next;
  }
  return *this;
}

List::~List()
{
  ListCell *p = First, *next;
  while (p != NULL)
  {
    next = p->Next;
    delete p;
    p = next;
  }
}

int List::IsIn(char c)
{
  ListCell* p = First;
  while (p != NULL)
```

```
  {
    if (p->contents == c) break;
    p = p->Next;
  }
  return p != NULL;
}

void List::remove(char c)
{
  ListCell *pl = First, *p2 = NULL;
  while (pl->contents != c)
  {
    p2 = pl;
    pl = pl->Next;
  }
  p2->Next = pl->Next;
  delete pl;
}

void main()
{
  List 11, 12;
  11.add('a');
  11.add('b');
  11.add('c');
  12 = 11;
  11.remove('b');
  cout << 11.IsIn('b') << 12.IsIn('c');
}
```

8.6 Class Nesting

The class `ListCell` in the previous example exists solely to aid in the implementation of the `List` class. It is meaningless outside of `List`, and programmers have no need to use it since the `List` class performs all the behaviors necessary for construction and manipulation of lists. Consequently, to enhance information hiding one might want to "hide" the entire `ListCell` class by enclosing it within the `protected` section of the `List` class. The syntax is outlined in the following example.

```
class List {
public:
//...exactly as before...
protected:

  class ListCell;
  class ListCell {
  friend List;
 public:
  //...exactly as before...
 protected:
  //...exactly as before...
 };

 ListCell* First;
};
```

Because class `ListCell` is defined within the `protected` section of `List`, it is not accessible outside of `List`, but the `List` class may use it as necessary.

Classes may also be defined within the `public` section of another class. In these cases, the inner class is globally accessible, but references to it must be qualified with the scope resolution operator. That is, if class `inner` is defined within the `public` section of class `outer`, `inner` can be referenced only by using the notation `outer::inner`.

Class nesting merely affects the scope of a class. It does not in any way modify the class member access rules. Therefore, `ListCell` must still declare class `List` as a `friend` in order to provide `List` access to its `protected` members.

If members of a nested class are not implemented inline, the scope resolution operator must be used twice when the method is defined.

```
{class outer
 ...
{class inner
  int a_method();
 ...
};
...
};

int outer::inner::a_method()
{
...
}
```

Type identifiers can also be defined within the scope of a class and either `public` or `protected` access can be provided, just as with nested classes. For example, the class below contains a publicly accessible enumerated type definition. External to the class, access to the enumerated constants must be qualified by the class name in which they are defined. The same would be true for any identifiers created by `typedef` statements within the `public` section of a class.

```
class code_table {
public:
 enum instruction {add, sub, mult,
 div, mov, cmp, jmp};
 ...
 int lookup(instruction op);
 ...
};

void main()
{
  code_table c;
  int i = c.lookup(code_table::mult);
}
```

Problem Solving Example:

Indicate which lines in the code below contain illegal references.

```
class A {
 friend class B;
public:
 void DoSomething();
protected:
 float x;
};

class B {
public:
 void DoSomething();
 float c;
protected:
 float y;
 class C {
 public:
  void DoSomething();
  float a;
 protected:
  float b;
 };
 C cObj;
};

void A::DoSomething()
{
 B bObj;
1.  bObj.c = 1.2;
2.  b.cObj.a = 4.5;
3.  bObj.y = 3.5;
}
```

```
        void B::DoSomething()
        {
         A aObj;
4.       cObj.a = 4.5;
5.       cObj.b = 1.2;
6.       aObj.x = 4.3;
        }

        void C::DoSomething()
        {
         A aObj;
         B bObj;
7.      bObj.y = 4.6;

        }
```

Lines 1 and 2 are incorrect because both `B::c` and `B::cObj` are `protected` members. The `friend` declaration in class `A` means that `B` can access the `protected` members of `A`, not that `A` can access the `protected` members of `B`.

Line 5 is incorrect because `C::b` is `protected`. The fact that class `C` is embedded in class `B` does not give `B` access to `protected` members of `C`.

Line 7 is incorrect because `B::y` is `protected`. The fact that `C` is embedded in `B` does not give `C` access to `protected` members of `B`.

8.7 `static` Class Members

Normally, every instance of a class contains individual instances of the class member attributes. For example, every `vehicle` object has individual `weight` and `wheels` variables. However, a class member that is declared as `static` is shared among all the instances of the class. Only one copy of a `static` class member exists regardless of how many instances of the class have been created.

`static` class members are often used to store data that is shared among all instances of a class. In these cases, duplicating the data in every object is wasteful. `static` members are also useful when there is information that must be communicated to all instances of a class—for example, a condition flag or a counter variable.

`static` member variables are declared within a class but must be explicitly allocated by a declaration statement with file level scope. For example, in VEHICLE.H one would write:

```
class Vehicle {
public:
  ...
protected:
  static int numberOfVehicles;
};
```

While in VEHICLE.CPP one would write:

```
#include "vehicle.h"

int Vehicle::numberOfVehicles = 0;

Vehicle::Vehicle()
{
  numberOfVehicles = numberOfVehicles + 1;
  ...
}
```

8.8 Type Conversion Methods

The code below defines a `fraction` class. Function overloading is used to provide several different constructor functions, and the multiplication operator is overloaded for fractions.

```
class fraction {
public:
  fraction(int top, int bot) :
    numerator(top), denominator(bot) {};
  fraction(int top) :
    numerator(top), denominator(1) {};
```

```
  fraction() :
    numerator(0), denominator(1) {};
protected:
  int numerator, denominator;
};

fraction operator *(fraction& f1,
                    fraction& f2)
{
  return fraction(f1.top()*f2.top(),
                  f1.bot()*f2.bot());
}
```

The constructor `fraction(int)` describes how to construct a fraction given an integer. It can also serve as a function for converting integers to fractions. In fact, it will be automatically used in this manner whenever the need arises.

```
fraction f1(2,3), f2;
f2 = f1 * 2; // f2 is now 4/3
```

In this example, the operand 2 is automatically converted to the fraction 2/1 using the `fraction(int)` constructor. Fraction multiplication is then performed. This constructor would also be invoked in the following situation.

```
void fn(fraction f)
{
  ... // do something
}

void main()
{
  int i;
  ...
  fn(i); // i will be converted to a
         // fraction and fn invoked
  ...
}
```

In this manner, constructor methods for a given class serve as functions that convert from some other class to that class.

It is also possible to specify type conversion in the opposite direction. For example, one may wish the system to be able to convert automatically from fractions to decimals. This can be accomplished by adding the following method to the fraction class.

```
class fraction {
public:
  ...
  operator float()
  {
    return (float) numerator /
           (float)denominator;
  };
protected:
  ...
};
```

A method of the form `class::operator type()` specifies an algorithm for converting a class object into a value of the specified type. In this case, a `fraction` is converted to a `float` by performing floating-point division on the numerator and denominator. Given this method, the following sequence can be performed.

```
fraction f1(2,3);
float x;
x = f1 + 0.2; // x is 0.866667
```

The automatic type conversions that one can create in C++ are a great convenience, but can also result in ambiguous expressions.

```
fraction f1(2,3), f2;
f2 = f1 * 2; // ambiguous conversion!
```

The second statement is ambiguous because the compiler is unable to decide whether to perform floating point (or decimal) or fraction multiplication. The solution is to use explicit typecasting.

```
f2 = f1 * (fraction) 2;
```

CHAPTER 9

Inheritance

9.1 Simple Inheritance

The inheritance mechanism allows a programmer to derive a new class type from an existing class type. Classes so created are called "derived" classes. The classes they are derived from are called "base" classes. For example, one may define a `truck` class to be a specific kind of `vehicle`.

```
class truck : public vehicle {
public:
  truck(float in_weight,
        int in_wheels = 4,
        float max_load = 24000.0)
  {
    wheels = in_wheels;
    weight = in_weight;
    payload = max_load;
  };

  float efficiency()
  { return payload / (payload + weight); };

  void honk()
```

```
  { cout << "Aooga!\n" };
protected:
  float payload;
};
```

The syntax `public vehicle` means that the `truck` class will inherit the variables and methods defined in the `vehicle` class. Thus, a `truck` object will have `wheels`, `weight`, and `payload` attributes, and `wheel_loading()`, `efficiency()`, and `honk()` methods. Just as `truck` is a derived class of `vehicle`, one could similarly define other derived classes of `vehicle`, derived classes of those derived classes, and so on, forming a hierarchy of data types.

Destructor, constructor, copy, and assignment methods are not inherited to derived classes and must be explicitly created if they are desired.

It is frequently useful for derived classes to redefine a method or attribute that is present in one of its base classes. `Trucks`, for example, have a distinctive `honk()` method. When a `truck` object receives a `honk()` message it will respond with "Aooga!" since that is the message specifically associated with `trucks`. Instances of other `vehicle` classes that do not have specific `honk()` methods may respond by displaying "Beep Beep!" after receiving a honk message. In general, when an object receives a message, it will search upward through its inheritance hierarchy until it finds a matching method, then execute that method.

9.2 Construction and Destruction of Derived Class Objects

An alternate way of defining the `truck()` constructor method would involve first invoking the `vehicle()` constructor, then performing any construction steps specific to `trucks`. The method definition below adopts this approach to `truck` construction.

```
truck(float in_weight,
      int in_wheels = 4,
      float max_load = 24000.0) :
```

```
vehicle(in_weight, in_wheels)
{
  payload = max_load;
}
```

The notation : *base class(arg1, arg2 ...)* following a constructor means "invoke the base constructor with the specified arguments."

If the base class constructor is not explicitly called in this way, the C++ compiler will automatically generate a call to the base class's default constructor (the constructor with no parameters) before the derived class's constructor is called. If the base class has no default constructor, the derived class will not compile. Thus, when a derived class object is created, the various relevant constructor methods are executed beginning with the topmost base class and proceeding down the inheritance hierarchy for each class on the inheritance path.

When a derived class object is destroyed, class destructors are automatically executed in the reverse order in which the constructors were executed.

Problem Solving Example:

Create a C++ inheritance hierarchy for animals as described below.

All animals have a name (a 32 byte character string). By default, when asked to talk, all animals print a message saying "I can't talk!". When asked if they can fly, by default all animals return a FALSE value. When asked their names, all animals print out their names.

Birds are animals that can fly.

Parrots are birds that have a vocabulary (a string of 64 characters) and can fly. When asked to talk, parrots print out their vocabulary.

```
class Animal {
public:
 Animal(char* s) {strcpy(name, s);};
 int CanFly() {return 0;};
```

```
 void Name() {cout << name;};
 void Talk() {cout << "I can't talk.";};
protected:
 char name[32];
};

class Bird: public Animal {
public:
 Bird(char* s): Animal(s) {};
 int CanFly() {return 1;};
};

class Parrot: public Bird {
public:
 Parrot(char* ns, char* vs): Bird(ns)
 {
  strcpy( vocabulary, vs);
 };
 void Talk() {cout << vocabulary;};
protected:
 char vocabulary[64];
};
```

9.3 Inheritance and Information Hiding

The keywords can also be used to control the inheritance mechanism when derived classes are created. As seen in the previous section, the usual method of specifying class derivation is to specify `public` *base_class* in the derived class definition. Using this technique, called `public` derivation, the `public` members of the base class become `public` members of the derived class and the `protected` members of the base class become `protected` members of the derived class. (`Private` members are never inherited.)

One may also specify `protected` or `private` derivation by writing `protected` *base_class* or `private` *base_class* after the derived class name. When `protected` derivation is used, the `public` and `protected` members of the base class become `protected` members of the derived class. Under `private` derivation, the `public` and `protected` members of the base class become `private` members of the derived class.

9.4 Multiple Inheritance

It is possible for a class to be derived from more than one base class. This situation is called multiple inheritance and is illustrated by the example below.

```
class rental_car : public vehicle {
public:
  rental_car(float in_rate,
             float in_weight,
             int in_wheels = 4)  :
  vehicle(in_weight, in_wheels)
  {
    daily_rate = in_rate;
  };

  float rate() {return daily_rate;};
protected:
  float daily_rate;
};

class driver {
public:
  driver(float in_rate) {hourly_rate = in_rate;};
  float rate() {return hourly_rate;};
protected:
  float hourly_rate;
};
class chauffeured_vehicle : public rental_car,
                            public driver {
```

```
public:
  chauffeured_vehicle(float vehicle_rate,
                      float driver_rate,
                      float in_weight,
                      int in_wheels = 4) :
  rental_car(vehicle_rate, in_weight, in_wheels),
  driver(driver_rate)
  {
  }

  float cost(float hours)
  {
    return hourly_rate*hours +
      ((int)(hours/24+0.5))*daily_rate;
  };
};
```

In this example, the chauffeured_vehicle class is derived from both rental_car and driver. Any chauffeured_vehicle object contains all the methods and attributes of vehicle, rental_car, driver, and chauffeured_vehicle.

When multiple inheritance occurs it is easily possible for the same identifier to be present in two or more of a class's base classes. In the example above, the chauffeured_vehicle class inherits a rate() method from both its base classes. Given cv as a chauffeured_vehicle object, the reference cv.rate() is therefore ambiguous. The scope resolution operator is used to resolve the ambiguous references in these cases. Using this operator, one could access cv.rental_car::rate() or cv.driver::rate().

Similar syntax is used to resolve ambiguous references to base class components within a class definition. For example, the cost() method could be written as:

```
 float cost(float hours)
{
```

```
  return driver::rate()*hours +
  ((int)(hours/24 + 0.5))*
  rental_car::rate();
}
```

9.5 `virtual` Methods and Polymorphism

Given the declaration `vehicle *p`, it is acceptable for `p` to point to either a `vehicle` object or a `truck` object since trucks are a derived class of vehicles. Since vehicles and trucks have different `honk()` methods, one would presumably like the expression `p->honk()` to print either "Beep! Beep!" or "Aooga" depending upon the class of object `p` is pointing to. This desired behavior is called "polymorphism."

However, by default, methods in C++ do *not* exhibit polymorphic behavior. Thus, if `p` is a pointer to a `vehicle` and given the class definitions of `vehicle` and `truck` seen earlier, the invocation `p->honk()` will always result in the execution of `vehicle::honk()` even if `p` happens to point to a `truck` object. To produce polymorphic behavior in a method, a C++ programmer must mark that method as being `virtual`, as shown below.

```
class vehicle {
public:
  virtual void honk()
    { cout << "Beep Beep!\n"; };
};

class truck : public vehicle {
 public:
 virtual void honk()
   { cout << "Aooga!\n"; };
};
```

The invocation of `virtual` methods requires a great deal of run-time overhead that is not required for invoking nonvirtual methods. This is why methods are not `virtual` by default. Programmers should consider carefully which methods require polymorphism and which do not.

Only those methods that require it should be marked as `virtual`.

The keyword `virtual` should appear only within a class definition. That is, if only the method's prototype is given in the class definition, the prototype should be marked as `virtual` but the implementation should not be. This is illustrated below.

```
class vehicle {
public:
  ...
// declare virtual in prototype
    virtual void honk();
  ...
protected:
  ...
};

// do not repeat the virtual keyword here
void vehicle::honk()
{
 cout << "Beep! Beep!";
}
```

Problem Solving Example:

Which methods in the `Animal` hierarchy should be preceded with the word `virtual`?

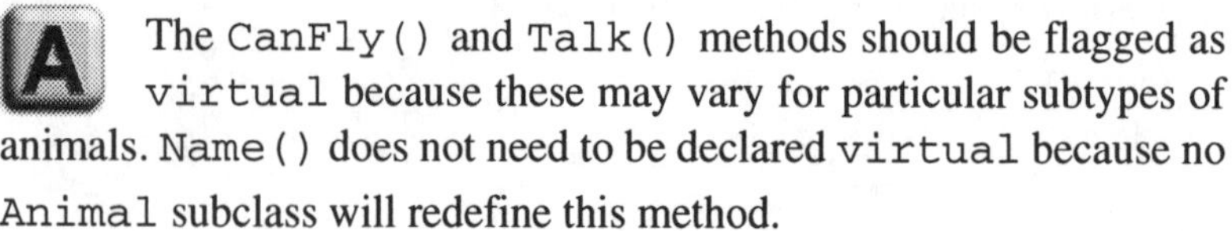

The `CanFly()` and `Talk()` methods should be flagged as `virtual` because these may vary for particular subtypes of animals. `Name()` does not need to be declared `virtual` because no `Animal` subclass will redefine this method.

9.6 Abstract Classes

A *pure* virtual *method* is defined using the notation:

virtual type name(arg1, arg2 ...) = 0;

A class with one or more pure `virtual` methods is called an "abstract" class. No objects of that class can be created. Abstract classes can only be used as a base class for another class. They are often used to create "schemas" which define a set of related classes.

```
class shape {
public:
   ...
   virtual draw() = 0;
   ...
};

class square : public shape {
public:
   ...
   virtual draw(); // square class MUST implement
                   // this method since it is a
pure
                   // function in its base class
   ...
};
```

Templates

10.1 Class Templates

Templates allow for the creation of generic program constructs. As the name suggests, templates do not define executable code, but define a form from which code can be generated. Templates must be *instantiated* to create usable program units (classes, functions, and so forth).

A template has the form *template<parameters> construct.* For example, the following defines a template for a `vector` class. In this example, `t` is a template parameter that represents the data type that is to be stored in the `vector`. The term `class` is somewhat misleading here. In this context, `class` means any C++ data type.

```
template<class t>
class vector {
public:
 vector(){contents = NULL;};
 vector(int in_size) : size(in_size)
    { contents = new t[size];};
 vector(int in_size, t initial_value);
 ~vector() { delete [] contents; };
// return reference to specified element
 t& operator [](int index);
```

```
protected:
 int size;
 t *contents;
};

//Note that each method implementation must be
//preceeded by its own template statement

template<class t>
vector<t>::vector(int in_size,
            t initial_value)
 : size(in_size)
{
 contents = new t[size];
 for (int i = 0; i <= size-1; ++i)
    contents[i] = initial_value;
}

template<class t>
t& vector<t>::operator [](int index)
{
 assert((index >= 0) && (index <= size));
 return contents[index];
}
```

The template is used to generate particular vector classes by specifying `vector<type>` in a declaration where `type` is a type identifier specifying the type of value to be stored in the vector. This notation causes the template to be instantiated for that particular type, in effect causing the compiler to generate a class definition by replacing the template parameter with the specified type identifier. The method is illustrated in the following example.

```
void main()
{
// a is a vector of integers
```

```
  vector<int> a(100);
// b is a vector of floats
  vector<float> b(50);
 ...
}
```

Since it is tedious to write `vector<type>` whenever a vector is declared, it is common practice to use a `typedef` statement to associate type identifiers with template instantiations, as shown below.

```
typedef vector<int> int_vector;
typedef vector<float> float_vector;
...
void main()
{
 int_vector a(100);
 float_vector b(50);
 ...
}
```

Since templates are definitions only and do not themselves cause object code to be generated, they should be placed in ".h" files when used as part of a larger program. That is, in the case of the vector template, both the class specification and the method implementations should be placed in the ".h" file.

A template identifier (`vector` for example) can never be written without the required template parameters. This is because there is no class called `vector`. Rather, `vector` is an outline from which a class can be generated. Therefore, in writing the implementation of the `vector` methods, it is necessary to write `vector<t>::operator [](int index)` and precede this by a statement specifying the template parameters.

Templates are very convenient, but programmers must be careful when using them. They may not be as generic as they seem. For example, the `vector` template will instantiate correctly only for data types for which the assignment operator is defined. This is because the assignment operator is used with a `t` type variable in the implementation of the "initial value" constructor method.

Since the assignment operator will not work with arrays, the following sequence would not compile:

```
typedef float matrix[100][100];
typedef vector<matrix, 50> // ERROR!
```

Should one wish to do this, the assignment operator must first be overloaded to work with `matrix` types.

Problem Solving Examples:

Turn the `Stack` class from the review question in Section 8.3.2 into a template.

```
#ifndef STACK_H
#define STACK_H

template<class T>
class Stack {
public:
 Stack(int size);
 ~Stack();
 void Push(T value);
 T Pop();
protected:
 T* contents;
 int top;
 int maxSize;
};

template<class T>
Stack::Stack(int size)
{
 contents = new T[size];
 top = -1;
 maxSize = size;
```

```
}
template<class T>
Stack::~Stack()
{
delete [] contents;
}
template<class T>
void Stack::Push(T value)
{
 ++top;
 contents[top] = value;
}
template<class T>
T Stack::Pop()
{
 T result = contents[top];
 --top;
 return result;
}
#endif
```

Q Show how to use the stack template by writing a program that reads three integers, pushes them, pops them off, and prints them, then reads three floats, pushes them on another stack, pops them off, and prints them.

A

```
#include "stack.ccp"
#include <iostream.h>
void main()
{
 Stack<int> s1(8);
```

```
Stack<float> s2(8);
int j, k;
float f;
for (j = 0; j < 3; ++j)
{
 cin >> k;
 s1.Push(k);
}
for (j = 0; j < 3; ++j)
  cout << s1.Pop();
for (j = 0; j < 3; ++j)
{
 cin >> f;
 s2.Push(f);
}
for (j = 0; j < 3; ++j)
  cout << s2.Pop();
}
```

10.2 Function Templates

Templates can also be used to write "generic" functions. For example, one could define a generic `sort()` function template:

```
template<class t>
void sort(t *a, int size)
{
  ...
  // insert your favorite sorting
  // algorithm here
 ...
}
```

The C++ compiler is intelligent enough to instantiate a function template automatically when it encounters a template function call.

Thus, given the preceding template, the following code sequence would be permissible:

```
int a[100];
float x[50];
...
// put some values in the arrays
...
sort(a, 100);
sort(x, 50);
```

The compiler realizes that the call sort(a,100) requires an instantiation of sort<int> and does so automatically. Similarly, the call sort(x, 50) causes an instantiation of the sort template with parameter float.

Function templates can have the same sort of hidden dependencies that class templates can have. For example, just as the vector <> template works only for classes for which assignment is defined, the sort template would presumably only work for data types for which the relevant comparison operator is defined (< or > depending upon how the sort is implemented).

10.3 Templates for Derived Classes

In order to illustrate the use of templates with derived classes, a subclass of vector is defined below which allows for the programmer to specify upper and lower bounds for the vector's indices.

```
template<class t>
class indexed_vector : public vector<t> {
public:
  indexed_vector() : upper(0), lower(0) {};
  indexed_vector(int first, int last) :
  vector<t>(last-first+1)
  {
    upper = first;
    lower = last;
  };
```

```
  indexed_vector(int first, int last, t value) :
  vector<t>(last-first+1, value)
  {
    upper = first;
    lower = last;
  };

  t& operator [](int index)
  {
    return vector<t>::operator [](index - lower);
  };
protected:
  int upper, lower;
};
```

10.4 Templates for Recursive Classes

The code below illustrates the use of templates in creating recursive structures; in this case, the `List` class seen earlier. Readers should again note that wherever a class name is required, a template parameter must be provided. A `typedef` is used in `List` to avoid the necessity of writing `ListCell<t>` whenever a reference to that class is needed.

```
template<class t>
class ListCell;

template<class t>
class ListCell {
 friend List<t>;
public:
  ListCell(t c, ListCell<t> *p = NULL)
   : contents(c), Next(p) {};

  ListCell<t>& operator =
   (const ListCell<t>& lc)
  {
```

```
    contents = lc.contents;
    Next = lc.Next;
    return *this;
  }

   t GetContents()
    {return contents;};
   ListCell<t>* GetNext()
    {return Next;};

  ~ListCell() {};
protected:
  t contents;
  ListCell<t>* Next;
};

template<class t>
class List {
 typedef ListCell<t> tCell;
public:
 List() {First = NULL;}

 List (const List<t>&);
 List<t>& operator =(List<t>& l)

 void add(t c)
  { First = new tCell(c, First); }
 void remove(t);
 int IsIn(t);

 ~List();
protected:
 tCell* First;
};

template<class t>
List<t>::List(const List<t>& l)
```

```
{
 if (l.First == NULL)
  First = NULL;
 else
 {
  First = new tCell(l.First->contents,
      NULL);
  tCell *p1 = l.First->Next;
  tCell *p2 = First;
  while (p1 != NULL)
  {
   cout << p1->contents;
   p2->Next = new tCell(p1->contents, NULL);
   p2 = p2->Next;
   p1 = p1->Next;
  }
 }
}

// and so on for other List<t> methods
```

Input and Output

11.1 Files and Streams

Input and output facilities are provided by the functions and objects defined within the IOSTREAM.H file, included with every C++ implementation. Programmers may also opt to perform I/O using the C library package, STDIO.H, but this usage is archaic and is not discussed here.

The `iostream` package provides access to standard input via the object `cin`, to standard output via the `cout` object, and to the standard error device via `cerr`. The symbol << is used to write to `cout` or `cerr` and the symbol >> is used to read from `cin`. Their use is illustrated below.

```
cout << "Please enter two integer values\n";
cin >> i >> j;
cout << "You entered " << i << ' '
     << j << " \nTheir sum is "
     << i + j << '\n';
```

The object `cin` skips over all white space (blanks, tabs, and newlines) when performing an >> operation. When reading an integer, it consumes a sign, if present, then consumes characters until a non-digit is encountered. Real numbers are read in an analogous manner.

Some examples are presented in Table 11.1. The table assumes `i` is an integer, `x` is a `float`, and `c` is a character.

The objects `cin`, `cout`, and `cerr` are all instances of the class `iostream`. In addition to the << and >> operators, there are a number of methods defined for `iostream` objects. These are summarized in Table 11.2.

The `width()` method can be used to set the output field width for `cout`. When the width is zero, as it is by default, values are printed with no leading spaces. If the width is set to a number larger than the number of digits to be written, the value is padded with the current fill character. The fill character is a space by default and may be set using the fill method. Note that when the width is set using the `width` method, it affects only the next output item. Afterward, the width automatically resets to zero.

TABLE 11.1
Examples Showing Effect of >> with `cin`

Input source	Effect of `cin >> i >> c >> x`
`123 a123`	`i` = 123 `c` = 'a' `x` = 123.0

`123`
`a`
`123.5`
	`i` = 123
	`c` = 'a'
	`x` = 123.5

`+123a.123`	`i` = 123 `c` = 'a' `x` = 0.123
`123aa123`	`i` = 123 `c` = 'a' `x` is undefined due to unexpected input
`a123 c123`	all variables undefined due to unexpected input when reading `i`

TABLE 11.2
Methods for `iostream` Objects

`char get()`	Read and return the next character, including whitespace characters
`put(char c)`	Output `c`
`read(char s[], int size)`	Read size number of characters and put them in `s`
`write(char s[], int size)`	Write size number of character from *s*
`getline(char s[], int n, char delim = '\n');`	Read at most `n` –1 characters until the `delim` character or `eof` is encountered. Put them in `s`, followed by the '`\0`' character
`width(int i)`	Set the output field width of `obj` to `i`
`precision(int i)`	Set the output precision of `obj` to `i`. This is the number of digits to write to the right of the decimal point.
`char fill(char c)`	Set the fill character to `c`
`int eof()`	Return true (1) if `obj` has attempted to read past the end of the file
`int bad()`	Return true if an illegal operation has been requested
`int fail()`	Return true if `obj.bad()` or if an operation has failed
`int good()`	Return true if none of the previous error conditions apply

Precision refers to the number of digits to print to the right of the decimal point. It is relevant only for `float` or `double` values. A number will be rounded to fit within the specified precision.

The `fail()` method is useful for testing if an operation was successful. In the following example it is used to determine if an integer was input properly.

```
cout << "Enter number of students";
cin >> n;
while (cin.fail())
{
 cout << "Try again please:";
 cin >> n;
}
```

In the following example, `eof()`, `get()`, and `put()` are used to copy an input source. Note that `eof()` does not become true until after a "read past end of file" operation has been attempted.

```
char c = cin.get();
while (!cin.eof())
{
 cout.put();
 c = cin.get();
}
```

11.2 Overloading the Stream Operators

It is common practice for C++ programmers to overload the << and >> operators when creating new data types. For example, given the `student_record` structure presented earlier, one would like to be able to produce code similar to that shown in the following example.

```
student_record r = {1234, 's', 3.25};
...
cout << s;
```

Doing so requires that the stream operators be overloaded to work with student records. The following example demonstrates this technique:

```
ostream& operator <<(ostream& out,
                     student_record& s)
{
  out << s.id << '\t' << s.classification << '\t'
      << s.gpa << '\n';
  return out;
}
```

When overloaded, the `iostream` operators << and >> should always return a reference to their left operand. This, and the fact that they are left associative, ensures that they can continue to be used in the manner of a stream. That is, given `cout << a << b << c`, left associativity ensures that the expression is evaluated as `(((cout << a) << b) << c)`. The fact that << yields a reference to its left operand, `cout`, ensures that after evaluating `(cout << a)` the expression effectively becomes `((cout << b) << c)`, and evaluation continues in the desired manner.

Problem Solving Example:

Overload the input and output stream operators for the `Fraction` structure defined in Section 5.6.

```
ostream& operator <<(ostream& operator out,
         Fraction& f)
{
out << f.numerator << '/' << f.denominator;
}

istream& operator >>(istream& operator in,
          Fraction& f)
{
char slash;
in >> f.numerator >> slash >> f.denominator;
}
```

11.3 Setting Format Options

Detailed formatting options for `iostream` objects can be controlled using the `setf()` method. This method modifies a set of bitflags (stored within a `long` variable) used by `iostream` objects to maintain the current state of their formatting options. The class `ios` defines constants that can be used in conjunction with `setf()` to access these bit fields. These constants are presented in the following table.

When called with one parameter, `setf()` has the effect of turning "on" the specified formatting option. When called with two parameters, the options specified by the second parameter are turned off, then the options specified by the first parameter are turned on. For example, the statement `cout.setf(ios::fixed, ios::floatfield)` causes the `ios::scientific` flag to be turned off and the `ios::fixed` flag to be turned on. All real numbers are subsequently displayed in fixed-point notation. The second argument is necessary to ensure that `ios::scientific` will be off, since both this and `ios::fixed` cannot be on at the same time. Similarly, the statement `cout.setf(ios::right, ios::adjustfield)` would be used to set output formatting to right justification. Note that the `basefield` flags affect only integer output.

TABLE 11.3
Format Flag Constants

`ios::skipws`	skip whitespace
`ios::left`	left justify
`ios::right`	right justify
`ios::internal`	pad after sign or base indicator
`ios::dec`	decimal output
`ios::oct`	octal output
`ios::hex`	hex output
`ios::showbase`	show base of output
`ios::showpoint`	force display of decimal point (floats only)
`ios::uppercase`	always display in upper case
`ios::showpos`	add "+" to front of positive numbers
`ios::scientific`	displays `floats` in scientific notation
`ios::fixed`	displays `floats` in fixed-point notation
`ios::unitbuf`	flush all streams after insertion
`ios::stdio`	flush `stdout`, `stderr` after insertion
`ios::basefield`	This is equal to: `ios::dec|ios::oct|ios::hex`
`ios::adjustfield`	This is equal to: `ios::left|ios::right|ios::internal`
`ios::floatfield`	This is equal to: `ios::scientific|ios::fixed`

Format flags can be combined using bitwise OR to create groups of formatting options. Thus, the call `cout.setf(ios::fixed|ios::showpos|ios::uppercase, ios::floatfield)` turns off `ios::scientific` and turns on `ios::fixed`, `ios::showpos`, and `ios::uppercase`.

Because most I/O operations are buffered, it is not always possible to rely upon the fact that, for example, a message will be displayed exactly when it is written to `cout`. Instead, on many systems, output is not written to the appropriate device until the output buffer is full. The `ios::unitbuf` flag allows the programmer to specify that all I/O buffers are to be emptied as soon as an item is inserted into them. The flag `ios::stdio` restricts this to the `cout` and `cerr` buffers.

Problem Solving Example:

Write a C++ program that reads an integer and prints it out twice in hexidecimal notation, right justified, with a field width of 12.

```
#include <iostream.h>

void main()
{
 int n;
 cin >> n;
//these settings are "permanent"
 cout.setf(ios::hex);
 cout.setf(ios::showbase);
 cout.setf(ios::right);
//this affects only the next << operation
 cout.width(12);
 cout << n;
//must reset the width
 cout.width(12);
 cout << n;
}
```

11.4 Formatting and Using I/O Manipulators

In addition to using `setf()`, formatting options can be controlled by including I/O *manipulators* in a stream. These are defined in the standard header file IOMANIP.H and summarized in the table below. Manipulators have the same effects as their corresponding `iostream` methods. An example illustrating their use is given in the following table.

TABLE 11.4
I/O Manipulators Defined in IOMANIP.H

`oct`	set ouput base to octal
`dec`	set output base to decimal
`hex`	set output base to hexidecimal
`endl`	send '`\n`' and flush stream
`ends`	send '`\0`' and flush stream
`flush`	flush stream
`ws`	ignore whitespace
`setbase(int)`	set output base to specified integer (8, 10, or 16)
`setfill(char)`	set fill character
`setw(int)`	set output width
`setprecision(int)`	set output precision
`resetiosflags(long)`	turn off specified `ios` flags
`setiosflags(long)`	turn on specified `ios` flags

The following program illustrates the usage of I/O manipulators:

```
#include <iostream.h>
#include <iomanip.h>

void main()
{
  cout
```

```
    << resetiosflags(ios::floatfield |
                          ios::adjustfield)
    << setiosflags(ios::fixed | ios::right)
    << setw(10) << setprecision(2)
    // output will now be right justified, floats
    // printed in fixed fields
       << 123.456 << endl
    // output is:  123.46
      << hex << 16 << endl
    // output is:10
      << setw(10) << setfill('#') << 123 << endl
    // output is:########7b
      << 123.456;
    // output is:123.46
}
```

Problem Solving Example:

Write the same program as in 11.3, but use I/O manipulators.

```
#include <iostream.h>
#include <iomanip.h>

void main()
{
 int n;
 cin >> n;
 cout << setiosflags(ios::right | ios::hex |
   ios::showbase) << setw(12) << n << setw(12)
  << n;
}
```

11.5 File Classes

The header file FSTREAM.H defines three file classes: `ifstream`, `ofstream`, and `fstream`. These are used for read-only files, write-only files, and read/write files respectively. The `open()` and `close()` methods are used to associate and disassociate physical files with file objects. This is illustrated by the example below, which copies one file to another.

```
ifstream infile;
ofstream outfile;
infile.open("infile.txt");
outfile.open("outfile.txt");
char c = infile.get();
while (!infile.eof())
{
  outfile.put(c);
  c = infile.get();
}
infile.close();
outfile.close();
```

Alternately, the file name for a file object can be specified as an argument to its constructor. Thus, one could also have written:

```
ifstream infile("infile.txt");
ofstream outfile("outfile.txt");
char c = infile.get();
...
```

Objects of class `fstream` may be used as either read files, write files, or read/write files. When creating an `fstream` object, one of the three file modes must be specified using the constants `ios::in`, `ios::out`, or `ios::in|ios::out`, as illustrated in the following example:

```
fstream read_only_file("infile.txt",
                         ios::in);
fstream write_only_file("outfile.txt",
                         ios::out);
fstream read_write_file("update.txt",
                         ios::in | ios::out);
```

One may also open a file in "append" mode by specifying `ios::app`.

The file classes maintain a file position marker that indicates the character position where the next I/O operation is to be performed. The methods `seekp()` and `seekg()` are used to modify this position marker for write and read files, respectively. The methods take two parameters. The first specifies an offset and the second specifies a starting point. Usually the second parameter is one of the values `ios::beg`, `ios::end`, `ios::cur`, which represent the beginning of the file, end of the file, and the current file position, respectively. Thus, given that `infile` is an object of type `ifstream`, the call `infile.seekg(-1,ios::cur)` has the effect of moving the file position marker back one character. Similarly, given that `outfile` is an `ofstream` object, the statement `outfile.seekp (0,ios::beg)` places the file position marker at the beginning of the file associated with `outfile`. The methods `tellp()` and `tellg()` can be used to determine the current file position marker specified as an offset from `ios::beg`.

The following program modifies a file by replacing all periods with exclamation marks.

```
#include <iostream.h>
#include <fstream.h>

void main()
{
 char fname[32];
 cout << "Enter file name: ";
```

```
cin >> fname;
fstream f(fname, ios::in | ios::out);
char c = f.get();
while (!f.eof())
{
  if (c == '.')
  {
   f.seekp(-1, ios::cur);
   f.put('!');
  }
  c = f.get();
}
}
```

11.6 Binary I/O

The preceding examples operated upon files by reading and writing individual characters. It is often convenient to read or write an entire sequence of bytes in one operation, for example, a vehicle object or a student record. The `read()` and `write()` methods are used for this purpose. These methods take two parameters: the first is an address specifying the location of the object to be read or written, and the second is an integer indicating the size of the object. The address parameter should be specified using the type cast `unsigned char *`. For example, the following sequence writes the binary image of a vehicle object into a file.

```
ofstream ofile("vehicles");
vehicle v(2000);
ofile.write((unsigned char *) &f,
             sizeof(vehicle));
```

Miscellaneous C++ Topics

12.1 Command Line Arguments

Although none of the previous examples has done so, it is possible for C++ `main` functions to specify parameters that correspond to the command line arguments specified when the C++ program is executed. Two parameters are required to access command line arguments. The first should be an integer called `argc` which represents the number of command line arguments specified. The second is an array of character strings called `argv`. This array will be initialized by the operating system so that `argv[0]` is the name of the command invoked (i.e., the name of the program as specified on the command line), `argv[1]` is the first command line argument, `arg[2]` the second command line argument, and so forth.

For example, consider the following program.

```
#include <iostream.h>
void main(int argc, char *argv[])
{
 cout << "Command invoked was: "
      << argv[0]; << '\n';
```

```
 cout << "Command line parameters were:\n";
 for (int i = 1; i < argc; ++i)
  cout << argv[i] << '\n';
}
```

Assuming this program was compiled into the executable file TEST, the command `test one two three` would result in the following output:

```
Command invoked was: test
Command line parameters were:
one
two
three
```

Problem Solving Example:

Write a C++ program which reads the name of a text file from the command line. It prints each word in the file, one word per line. Words are separated by exactly one blank. Assume no line in the file will be longer than 80 characters.

A

```
#include <fstream.h>
#include <string.h>

void printwords(char* s)
{
 char* delim = " ";
 char* tok = strtok(s, delim);
 while (tok != NULL)
 {
  cout << tok << '\n';
  tok = strtok(NULL,delim);
 }
}
void main(int argc, char* argv[])
{
```

```
    ifstream in(argv[1]);
    char line[80];
    do
    {
     in.getline(line, 80);
     printwords(line);
    } while (! in.eof());
  }
```

12.2 Functions with a Variable Number of Arguments

C++ allows the specification of functions which take a variable number of arguments, provided that at least one fixed argument is given. The notation

type name(type arg1, ...)

specifies a function that takes at least one argument. The ellipses notation specifies that a variable number of arguments may be specified following the previous arguments.

Some means of identifying the number of arguments sent to a function must be provided by the programmer. Two means are traditionally adopted. Either the function is designed so that its first parameter is the number of arguments that will be specified, or the argument list is terminated by a special value indicating the end of the argument list. Both means are used in the examples to follow.

A set of macros defined in the file STDARG.H provides the means for accessing the arguments sent to such a function with a variable number of arguments. These macros are summarized in the following table.

TABLE 12.1
Macros

`va_list`	Used to define a pointer to the argument list provided to a function
`va_start(va_list, lastfix)`	Used to initialize the argument list for processing. `lastfix` should be the name of the last fixed argument provided to the function.
`va_arg(va_list, type)`	Used to get the next argument
`va_end(va_list)`	Used to "clean up" the argument list after it has been processed

The technique used for accessing the argument list is the same in both functions. First, a variable representing the argument list is declared using the `va_list` macro. Next, the argument list is initialized for processing by calling the `va_start` macro. The first parameter to this macro should be the argument list pointer variable and the second should be the name of the last fixed argument provided to the function. After `va_start` has been executed, each successive argument is accessed using `va_arg`. Each time this is called, it returns the "next" argument. The function `max1()` stops calling `va_arg` when it has processed the required number of arguments, while `max2()` stops when it encounters an argument of zero.

The second parameter to `va_arg` should be the type of the current argument. This is so that it knows how far to advance the argument pointer so that it points to the next argument. In the examples provided, all arguments are of type `int`. However, should one wish to design a function in which the number as well as types of arguments may vary, considerable complication will result.

The following program illustrates the use of variable arguments in C++.

```
#include <iostream.h>
#include <stdarg.h>
```

```
int max1(int argcnt, ...)
// function to select maximum of set of integer
//arguments
// argcnt specifies number of arguments
{
//arguments point to argument list
 va_list arguments;
//setup for argument list processing
 va_start(arguments, argcnt);

//current_max is first of the variable
//arguments
 int next_arg;
 int current_max = va_arg(arguments, int);

// process remaining arguments
 for (int i = 1; i <= argcnt-1; ++i)
 {
   // get next argument
   next_arg = va_arg(arguments, int);
   if (next_arg > current_max)
     current_max = next_arg;
 }
 return current_max;
}

int max2(int arg1, ...)
// function to select maximum of set of integer
// arguments terminated by 0
{
 va_list arguments;
 va_start(arguments, arg1);
 int next_arg = arg1;
 int current_max = arg1;

// process remaining arguments
```

```
 while (next_arg != 0)
 {
   if (next_arg > current_max)
     current_max = next_arg;
   next_arg = va_arg(arguments, int);
 }
 return current_max;
}

void main()
{
 cout << max1(3, 4, 5, 2) << '\t'
      << max1(2,4,3) << '\t'
      << max1(5, 1, 3, 4, 1, 2);
 //output will be: 5 4 4
 cout << max2(4, 5, 2, 0) << '\t'
      << max2(4,3,0) << '\t'
      << max2(1, 3, 4, 1, 2, 0);
 //output will be: 5 4 4
}
```

12.3 Function Pointers

```
int (*int_fn)(int, int)
```

The preceding statement defines `int_fn` as a pointer to a function that takes two integer arguments and returns an integer value. Given some function fitting that description such as,

```
int max(int a, int b)
{
 if (a > b)
    return a;
 else
```

```
  return b;
}
```

int_ fn can be made to point to that function by the statement int_ fn = &max. Alternately, one may omit the address operator, so that the statement int_ fn = max has the same effect. To execute the function pointed to by int_ fn one writes a statement such as:

```
cout << (*int_fn)(5, 10).
```

In general, the notation *return_type (*name)(type, type, ...)* defines *name* to be a pointer to a function of the specified *return_type* that takes parameters of the specified number and type. The function is called using the notation

*(*name)(arg, arg, ...).*

The typedef statement is often useful when using pointers to functions. Thus, rather than having to continually repeat *int (* name)(int, int)* every time one wishes to define a pointer to this sort of function, one could create a type identifier called int_ fn to represent "pointers to integer functions that take two integer parameters:"

```
typedef int (*int_fn)(int, int);
```

or,

```
typedef float (*float_fn)(float)
```

to represent "pointers to float functions that take a single float parameter."

Pointers to functions are used most often when a function needs the name of a function as a parameter. This is illustrated in the following example.

```
float poly1(float x)
{
 return x*x + 2*x + 1;
}

float poly2(float x)
{
```

```
 return x*x*x + 3*x*x * 4;
}

void chart(float_fn fn, float start,
           float end, float inc)
{
 for(float x = start; x <= end;
     x = x + inc)
   cout << x << fn(x) << '\n';
}

void main()
{
 chart(&poly1, 0.0, 1.0, 0.1);
 chart(&poly2, 0.0, 1.0, 0.1);
}
```

One can envision functions similar to `chart()` that compute the area under the curve of a specified polynomial for a specified interval or a function that plots a given polynomial on a graphics device.

12.4 Exception Handling

The keyword `try` defines a block of code in which errors can be intercepted and processed by programmer-specified exception handling routines, specified by the keyword `catch`. The general form of a `catch`/`try` code segment is outlined below.

```
try {
 //do something
}
catch (exception-object) {
//handle this type of exception
}
catch (exception-object) {
//handle this type of exception
}
//more catch blocks as needed
```

When an error is detected in the `try` block, an exception object of the appropriate class is "thrown" using the `throw` operator. Control is then transferred to the nearest `catch` block that is specified as catching that class of exception object. If no such catch block can be found, the program terminates in the usual manner.

The nearest `catch` block is located by back-tracking through the sequence of function calls that led to the function in which the throw statement was executed. After the `catch` block is executed, control is transferred to the next statement at the end of all related `catch` blocks, rather like executing a `break` statement within a `switch` construct. The technique is illustrated in the following example.

```
class MathErr {
public:
 MathErr(char *s) {strcpy(msg, s);};
 char msg[80];
};

class IOErr {
public:
 IOErr(char *s) {strcpy(msg, s);};
  char msg[80];
};

void io_stuff()
{
 ofstream outfile("out.txt");
 if (outfile.fail())
    throw(IOErr("File open error");
 //... do some stuff
 outfile.close();
}

void math_stuff()
{
  float x, y;
```

```
  cin >> x >> y;
  if (y == 0)
    throw(MathErr("Divide by zero"));
  cout << x / y;
  io_stuff();
}

void main()
{
 //any error outside of try block causes
 //program termination in the default manner
 try {
 //MathErr or IOErr objects that are "thrown"
 //will cause control to jump to
 //the appropriate catch block below
  math_stuff();
 }
 catch (MathErr& merror) {
  cout << "Program aborted due to math error: "
       << merror.msg << '\n';
 }
 catch (IOErr& ioerror) {
  cout << "Program aborted due to IO error: "
       << ioerror.msg << '\n';
 }
//control is transferred here after any of the
//above catch blocks are executed
}
```

Problem Solving Example:

Add code to the stack class files from Section 8.3.2 so that the function `Push()` will throw an `Overflow` object if an attempt is made to push onto a full stack and the function `Pop()` will throw an `Underflow` object if an attempt is made to pop from an empty stack. Implement a test program that shows how to catch these exception objects. The `Overflow` object should contain the value that caused the overflow.

The file STACK.H is:

```
#ifndef STACK_H
#define STACK_H

class Overflow {
public:
 Overflow(int n){value = n;};
 int value;
};

class Underflow {
public:
 Underflow(){};
};

class Stack {
public:
 Stack(int size);
 ~Stack();
 void Push(int value);
 int Pop();
protected:
 int* contents;
 int top;
```

```
int maxSize:
};
#endif
```

The file STACK.CPP looks like:

```
#include "stack.h"

Stack::Stack(int size)
{
 contents = new int[size];
 top = -1;
 maxSize = size;
}

Stack::~Stack()
{
 delete [] contents;
}

void Stack::Push(int value)
{
 if (top == maxSize - 1) throw
 Overflow(value);
 ++top;
 contents[top] = value;
}

int Stack::Pop()
{
 if (top == -1) throw Underflow();
 int result = contents[top];
 --top;
 return result;
}
```

The test program looks like:

```
#include "stack.h"
#include <iostream.h>
void main()
{
 Stack s(32);
 int i;
 try {
  i = s.Pop();
 }
 catch (Underflow)
 {
  cout << "Underflow thrown.\n";
 }
 try {
  for(i = 1;i < 100; ++i)
   s.Push(i);
 }
 catch (Overflow o)
 {
  cout << "Overflow thrown at:" << i;
 }
}
```

12.5 String Streams

The file STRSTREAM.H provides facilities that allow programmers to treat character strings as input and output streams. It defines two classes: `ostrstream` and `istrstream`. The former is used to write to strings, the latter to read from strings. Their use is illustrated here.

```
#include <iostream.h>
#include <strstream.h>

void main()
```

```
{
  char obuf[32] = "\0";
  int i = 42;
  ostrstream ostr(obuf, 32);
  ostr << "The value of i is " << i;
  // obuf is now the string "The value of i
  // is 42";
  cout << obuf;
  char* ibuf = "1234";
  istrstream istr(ibuf, 4);
  istr >> i; // i is now 1234
  cout << i;
}
```

12.6 The void* type

The void* type is designed to be compatible with any pointer type. void pointers cannot be referenced without explicit type casting. void pointers are usually used to specify function parameters that represent machine addresses. The example below uses the void* data type to implement a function that copies a block of memory.

void pointers are considered archaic by most authors and should be avoided if possible. Most problems for which one is tempted to use void pointers could be more reliably solved using templates.

```
#include <iostream.h>

void copy(void *a, void *b, unsigned int size)
//copy size number of bytes from address a
//to address b
{
   for (int = 1; i <= size; ++i)
   {
//void pointers must be typecast
   *(char*)b=*(char*)a;
```

```
//characters are single bytes
   ++(char*)a;
   ++(char*)b;
}
}
void main()
{
 int i=5;j=0;
 copy(&i,&j,sizeof(int));
 cout << j;
 double x=3.14,y=0;
 copy(&x,&y,sizeof(double));
 cout << y;
}
```